W9-AFJ-898

Set in Century Schoolbook 11/12
Sats: Alfabeta as, Halden
Printed by Tangen Grafisk Senter A/S, Drammen
Reproduction: Reproman A/B and Litorapid A/B
Gothenburg (theme sections) and Kopio-offset OY,
Helsinki (other illustrations)

Graphic design: Roland Thorbjörnsson (theme sections) and Lisa Wagle (other pages). Maps on pp. 12 and
45 engraved by Ellen Elkjær and Design Eide A/S.

Editor: Jan Ivar Haugen
Illustration editors: Ivar Libæk and Øivind
Stenersen

ISBN 82-504-1852-2
Copyright © Grøndahl & Søn Forlag A/S, Oslo 1991

This book has been published with the support of the
Norwegian Non-Fiction Authors' Fund.
The theme sections were prepared with the support of:
Norwegian Post Office Stamp Bureau
Helikopter Service A/S
The Norwegian Defence Forces
The Norwegian Shipowners' Association

Illustrations on the introductory pages:

p. 1: Woodcarving of Odin from the Old Town, Oslo
p. 3: Harald Sohlberg: Street in Røros 1903
pp. 4–5: Rock carving from Alta
p. 6: The Urnes portal
p. 7: Nils Aas: Statue of King Håkon VII.
p. 8: A Bell 212 of Norway's leading helicopter
    company, Helikopter Service A/S, landing on
    the diving ship «Arctic Seal» on the Ekofisk
    field in the North Sea

Røros, Urnes stave church and the rock carvings at
Alta are all on UNESCO's World Heritage List

HISTORY OF NORWAY

IVAR LIBÆK · ØIVIND STENERSEN

HISTORY OF NORWAY

FROM THE ICE AGE TO THE OIL AGE

Translated by
JOAN FUGLESANG AND VIRGINIA SIGER

GRØNDAHL & SØN FORLAG A.S

CONTENTS

STONE, BRONZE, AND IRON AGES

THE VIKING AGE 800–1030

THE MIDDLE AGES 1030–1537

NORWAY IN UNION WITH DENMARK 1537–1814

1814 – INDEPENDENCE AND A NEW UNION

NORWAY 1814–1905

PREFACE

The authors of this book had a desire to make Norway better known to a wider, international public. A number of surveys in recent years have shown that foreigners have very little knowledge of our country. Since it has been translated into English, German, French and Spanish, this book may help improve the situation.

One of our main aims has been to present Norwegian history from the earliest time to the present day with emphasis on those things that are particularly Norwegian; however, the book also describes Norway's international ties and involvement through the ages. It introduces the great personalities who have influenced both their own period and later generations – Saint Olav, Christian IV, Christian Frederik, Håkon VII and Einar Gerhardsen. But the masses are here too – the thousands of unknown men and women who for generations have built this country on the periphery of the world.

The rich illustrations show characteristics of Norwegian art, society and commercial life. The nineteen theme sections present historical development in selected areas. The combination of texts, illustrations, maps and diagrams helps the reader to acquire knowledge in a new, easily understood way.

The publishers have employed one of Scandinavia's best graphic designers, Swedish illustrator Roland Thorbjörnsson, to design the theme sections. He has made use of the latest computer technology and graphic production techniques for layout, cartography and computer graphics. Most of the watercolours in the theme sections were painted by Ulf Söderqvist. The other artists were Lennart Molin and Lars Jödahl.

The authors also acted as illustration editors and are responsible for the content of the theme sections. The idea and text for the theme «A Golden Age in Literature» are Anne Skalleberg's.

The book is based on important works by Norwegian historians. We are deeply grateful to all of them. We should also like to thank museums and archives all over the country for their valuable assistance. Special thanks are due to Professor Tarald Rasmussen for his help with the text on the Norwegian missionaries in the 19th century.

Ivar Libæk   *Øivind Stenersen*

STONE, BRONZE AND IRON AGES

The Stone Age (10,000–1800 B.C)

A clear winter morning a group of hunters stood on the shore of the European mainland and gazed northward across the frozen sea. A herd of reindeer was disappearing over the horizon. Should they dare follow them, the huntsmen wondered. The decision was easy. If the ice could sustain the weight of the reindeer, it was strong enough to take human beings, too.

As they made their way northwards, the huntsmen caught sight of an enormous glacier in the distance. When they came closer they noticed a narrow coastal strip in front of it. They encamped on the ice that night and went ashore the following day.

This is how we can imagine the arrival of the first men on the coast of Norway, somewhere between today's Arendal and Bergen, at a time towards the end of the Ice Age. For, when the climate became milder and the great glacier which had covered Scandinavia for thousands of years retreated, this southern part of Norway was the first to emerge.

In recent years, archaeologists have found flint weapons and implements which tell us about the first migrants to Norway. The earliest definite traces of humans excavated so far are from Rennesøy near Stavanger and date from the 10th millennium B.C.

At that stage there was dry land between Denmark and England, and the Viking Bank was an island out in the North Sea. Only a narrow strait, the Norwegian Trench, separated the Norwegian coast from the European mainland to the south, and in winter the sea froze over, making it easy for animals and humans alike to move north across it.

The first hunter-gatherers who came to Norway were part of the so-called Ahrensburg culture which flourished on the north German plains between 11,000 and 8000 B.C. As the temperature rose, these areas became covered with forest. The herds of reindeer trekked north towards the ice-cap of the Scandinavian interior, and some of the hunters and their families followed.

On their habitation sites we can find arrow-heads and other sharp pieces of flint which they used as axes, knives and augers. Sometimes there are signs of tents and fires. All the evidence suggests that these hunter people lived in small groups and moved frequently. Probably they had light tents and boats made of animal skins which enabled them to range over large distances. Traces of them have been found as far out as the Viking Bank.

By about 7000 B.C. the whole of present-day Norway was free of ice. People settled along the coast all the way up to the Kola peninsula. In the southern part of Norway and the county of Nordland the finds

Bear-hunting scene from the Alta rock carvings, c. 4200–3600 B.C.

Opposite page: There are still large flocks of wild reindeer in the Norwegian mountains.

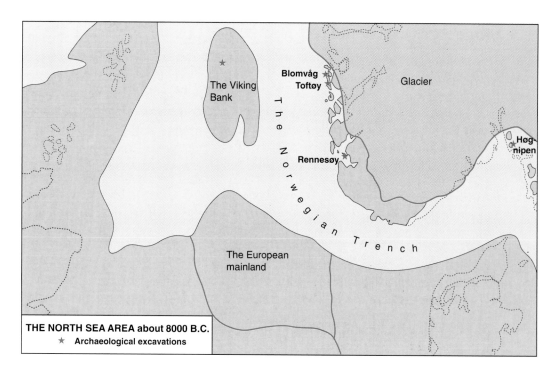

THE NORTH SEA AREA about 8000 B.C.
★ Archaeological excavations

dating from the early Stone Age are known as the Fosna culture, while in relation to the northern counties of Troms and Finnmark the name the Komsa culture is used.

The Komsa culture remained unchanged until about 4000 B.C., when new implements and pottery came into use. Excavated examples reveal close contact at this stage with hunter-gatherer societies in northern Sweden and Finland.

In southern Norway the Nøstvet culture replaced the Fosna culture around 7000 B.C. The climate of large parts of Norway became similar to that of southern England today, and the Nøstvet hunters took to using different tools and weapons because their natural environment was changing. Deciduous trees like alder, elm, hazel and oak superseded pine forests. To fell trees the Nøstvet men made large stone axes from hard rock. Most settlements were in sheltered inlets along the coast, where fish and seals were caught among the skerries. In the nearby forests there were deer, boars, bears and elks, while some hunters went inland to mountainous areas in search of reindeer and to fish trout. It is probable that hunting was chiefly a male responsibility and that the women and children stayed near the settle-

This beautiful battle-axe was found in the Fiskum Lake in Buskerud. It was probably sacrificed to the gods.

These bronze wind instruments (lurs) were found in a bog outside Stavanger. They were used for religious ceremonies.

ments, gathering firewood, edible roots, berries, shells and birds' eggs.

The first evidence of agriculture dates from around 4000 B.C. and has been found near the Oslo Fjord and Lake Mjøsa, and outside Bergen. Perhaps it was from farmers in Denmark and Sweden that the hunter-gatherer population learnt to keep domestic animals and cultivate corn. It is also possible that newcomers from the south brought farming with them.

Hunting and fishing remained the principal means of livelihood until the mid-21st century B.C. The subject-matter of drawings carved into flat surfaces of rock suggests this. However, more and more people took to keeping livestock and began burning down forests to sow corn in the ashes. When the soil was exhausted, they moved.

During the final six centuries of the Stone Age, which is reckoned as having ended about 1800 B.C., farming became the most significant occupation in southern Norway. Around this time the Battleaxe people arrived, and they may have brought with them the Indo-European language. Norwegian and most other European languages derive from this proto-Indo-European.

The Bronze Age (1800–500 B.C.)

Archaeologists have unearthed remains of early Bronze Age farms. These belonged to a rich upper class who lived in the best arable areas. They bartered with Danish chieftains, receiving weapons, jewellery and implements of bronze in exchange for furs and soapstone.

The majority of people continued to use implements and weapons of stone, bone and wood; yet farming and daily life underwent significant changes. During the Bronze Age it became usual to plough fields with a horse and primitive plough, and many farmers built larger houses. Women learnt to spin and weave, with the result that people no longer wore animal skins but dressed in cloth made of wool.

Valuable information about the Bronze Age is provided by the mighty burial mounds erected at the time, and by the many rock carvings. These drawings on flat rock surfaces depict people engaged in religious rituals whose purpose was to make fields, animals and humans more fruitful.

The Iron Age (500 B.C.–A.D. 800)

After about 500 B.C., the climate turned damper and colder, until it was roughly like today's. In western and northern Norway deciduous trees were superseded by pine and birch. In south-eastern Norway great spruce forests grew.

These climatic changes meant that the farmers had to build more homes to provide shelter and warmth for people and animals. Domestic animals had to spend the winter indoors now and so hay, bark and leaves were collected as winter fodder. The new buildings were preferably placed on morainal ridges where the soil was dry and sandy, and in many rural areas in Norway we still find the best and biggest farms in such locations. Their simple names are a clue to the physical conditions: Ås (ridge), Haug (hill), Åker (field) or Sander (sandy ridge) occur frequently.

Also at this time, knowledge of iron reached Scandinavia from the Celtic peoples of central Europe. Thus iron found in bogs up and down the country began to be smelted and forged into knives, scythes, axes and other tools.

Iron tools made cultivating the soil easier. Harvests became copious. The population increased. And more land was cleared for more farms.

On the earliest Iron Age farms several generations lived under one roof. When the sons married they, their wives and children continued living there as part of the extended family. All were subject to the head of the family, who ruled on the farm and was worshipped as a god after his death. Jointly the family owned the farm, and gave security and protection to all

This is how artist Else Lauvanger imagines life might have been in an Iron Age house.

who belonged to it. Every member could count on help in sickness and old age, or in case of conflict outside the family.

When the number of people living on one farm made it difficult to provide enough food for everyone, the youngest sons had to move out and clear land for new farms in the vicinity. In this way settlements arose. People of the same settlement would cooperate in various situations. If they were attacked by enemies, they warned one another by lighting fires on ridge tops. They also constructed simple forts, where they could seek refuge until the enemy had moved on.

When murder, theft or boundary disputes caused dissension between families in a settlement, all the freemen assembled at the *ting,* a sacred place where the use of force was forbidden. Many disputes settled at such assemblies ended in one person paying compensation to another, usually in the form of corn, butter or cattle. In a serious case the wrongdoer could be outlawed, which meant that all other freemen were at liberty to kill him.

A sense of community within a settlement was also provided by religious practices such as rituals arranged in honour of fertility gods, and the building of burial mounds when leading figures died.

In the first few centuries A.D. the extended families with the largest farms became increasingly wealthy and powerful. They had trading connections with the Roman Empire, and, later, with the Franks and other European peoples. Their graves have revealed splendid gold and silver jewellery, bronze pots, glass and weapons, items they presumably had acquired by bartering furs, down, animal skins and slaves.

The people of several settlements in a particular district (*rike* or *land*) were a tribe, and a tribe was ruled by a chief. The present-day names of certain parts of the country, Rogaland and Ringerike for example, are vestiges of such districts.

The chiefs performed the duties of priests at the ceremonies held in honour

of the gods. Sacrifices were made. And the freemen brought tributes to the chiefs, goods from their farms. With some of these gifts the chief paid his professional warriors or *hird,* by virtue of whom he was able to strengthen his authority over the local population. When he appeared at the assemblies with such a retinue, the farmers had little choice but to submit to him. A chief's *hird* could also be used to subjugate other tribes.

Gold amulets like this were made in the first centuries AD. This one from Vestfold is of particularly fine quality.

THE VIKING
AGE 800-1030

Gravestone from the Lindisfarne monastery, showing an attack by a band of Vikings.

Opposite page: Head from the famous Oseberg cart, showing how frightening the Vikings may have looked.

«In the same year the pagans from the northern regions came with a naval force to Britain like stinging hornets and spread on all sides like fearful wolves; robbed, tore and slaughtered not only beasts of burden, sheep and oxen, but even priests and deacons and companies of monks and nuns. And they came to the church of Lindisfarne, laid everything waste with grievous plundering, trampled the holy places with polluted steps, dug up the altars and seized all the treasures of the holy church. They killed some of the brothers, took away some with them in fetters...»

With these words an English monk described the sack of the monastery at Lindisfarne off the north-east coast of England in 793. Many reckon this event as the start of the Viking period. From the end of the 8th century until the mid 11th century, Scandinavians for the first time played a principal role in European history. Swedish, Danish and Norwegian Vikings set off on voyages to distant lands and coasts. They reached as far afield as the plains of Russia in the east, the Mediterranean and the Black Sea in the south, the Barents Sea in the north, and America in the west.

The name Viking is perhaps related to the Norwegian word *vik* meaning creek. Often the Vikings lurked in inlets and bays with their ships. In Byzantium they were known as Varangians, the Slavs used the term Rus, the English called them Danes while in France they were the Northmen.

Nowadays we do not look on the Vikings as merely murderers and pillagers. A many-faceted picture of the Vikings has been presented by recent archaeological excavations and work on European and Arab written sources. Emphasis is now placed on the Vikings as skilled shipbuilders, craftsmen, seafarers, explorers and merchants. They colonised large areas, founded towns and established new states.

It is also evident that to plunder and crush other peoples was a common occupation in the whole of Europe at that time. The Franks subjugated Saxons and Frisians, the Anglo-Saxons wrought havoc in Wales, and the Arabs looted in Spain. An important reason for the Vikings' poor reputation is the bad press they had from churchmen. Priests and monks were among the literate minority in those days, and they were not sparing in their criticism when churches and monasteries were attacked and robbed by men of another faith.

Causes of the Viking Activity Overseas

The longship symbolises the Viking Age. It represents the climax of the Vikings' technical achievements. With their mighty keel, flexible hull and efficient sails, these ships enabled the Vikings to cross long stretches of open sea in all kinds of weather. Even though the ships had low freeboards midships they could carry considerable cargoes, and because they were not deep of draught they could be rowed up shallow rivers. They could be beached on sandy shores, and if necessary rolled on logs from one river to another and past waterfalls. With such ships the Vikings could move fast, attack unexpectedly and retreat swiftly.

We stated earlier that when iron tools came into general use the population increased. Land was cleared for new farms. By the close of the 8th century there was a shortfall of arable land in western Norway, and this must have been the principal reason why people left that part of the country and crossed the sea to the thinly populated Shetlands, Orkneys, Faroes and Hebrides.

Many Vikings set off to seek wealth by trading. During the Viking Age new trade routes through Scandinavia developed, linking western Europe to the Byzantine Empire and the Caliphate in Baghdad. Swedish Vikings established bases along

The Oseberg ship was excavated in Vestfold in 1904. Today it stands in the Viking Skip Museum at Bygdøy, Oslo.

The Viking sword on the left is from Steinsvik, Lødingen in Nordland. The sword on the right is from Kongsgården in Åsnes, Hedmark.

the rivers of Russia and forced the local population to pay them tribute in the form of slaves and furs. They then sold these goods to the Arabs in exchange for silver coins, silk and other luxuries.

The trading place Birka on Lake Mälaren in Sweden was an important centre for eastern trade. Birka had close connections with Hedeby in Denmark, which was the economic hub of Scandinavia in the Viking period. From Hedeby there were trade routes to the Frankish Empire, to the British Isles and northward to Skiringssal in the Norwegian district of Vestfold.

In the 9th century, Skiringssal (or Kaupang) was the principal trading place in Norway. Archaeological finds made there give us interesting glimpses of its activity. Among imported items are Arabic coins, Frankish glass, and jewellery from Ireland. There is also evidence of crafts and industries: smiths, makers of glass

*This helmet from Gjer-
mundbu, Ringerike,
belies the myth that the
Vikings had
horned helmets.*

organisation, too, was effective, feared and admired. Their bands of warriors led by chiefs scorned death and had a high regard for strength, bravery, skill with weapons, and self-sacrifice. They worshipped the god of war Odin who, they believed, could decide defeat or victory on the battlefield. For a Viking it was preferable to die honourably doing battle for his chief than to die an old man in his own bed.

The Vikings believed that if they were killed in battle Odin would lead them to the heavenly kingdom Valhalla. There they could fight all day, and every evening be served meat and mead by beautiful women. This optimistic view of death may well have given the Vikings a psychological advantage over Christians in war. For in the churches the priests preached to people that after their death they might have to face the worst option and suffer eternal punishment in Satan's Hell.

Norwegian Expansion in the Viking Age

Though the Norwegians tended to head westward to the islands in the Atlantic, they also participated with Swedes and Danes in expeditions along the rivers of Russia and to western Europe. Often Vikings quarrelled with one another, and they were quite capable of allying themselves with Christian princes against other Vikings. On several occasions chiefs from various parts of Scandinavia united in large armies to conquer a particularly rich town or large territory.

Early in the 9th century it was the Viking habit to make small raids along coasts and rivers, and this remained an important feature of Viking tactics. However, from about the middle of the 9th century they began wintering on islands conveniently situated for further operations. In 843, for example, Vikings from Vestfold attacked Nantes in the Frankish Empire. They looted and set fire to the town, and then proceeded to build a base for themselves on the island of Noirmoutier near the estuary of the River Loire. From

beads, and goldsmiths had workshops. Pots, spindle whorls and soapstone moulds were significant export items, as were iron tools and iron ingots. We may also assume that domestic animals, grain, salt, wine, furs, weapons and slaves were traded. Many of the slaves would have been captured in raids like the one at Lindisfarne described above.

It seems that at the beginning of the Viking era the Scandinavians set off on their voyages purely for the purpose of trade, but on their travels they discovered conditions favourable to plunder. In the first place they must have realised the superiority of their ships, and that coasts were poorly defended. Further they saw how easy it was to steal silver and gold items from churches and monasteries. Once they were back home again, such news spread fast and tempted others out on raids.

It was not only their ships that made the Vikings a military threat. Their military

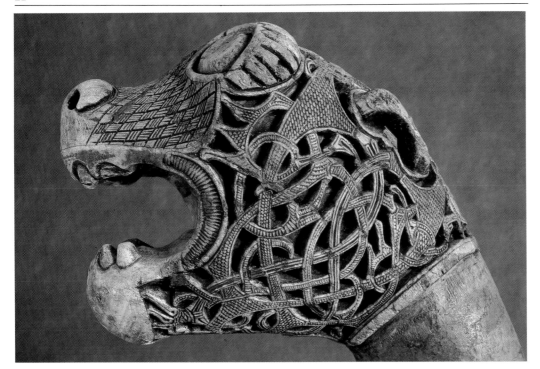

The head of a monster from the Oseberg find is a fine example of the high quality of wood-carving in the Viking Age.

there they undertook raids inland, and forced the inhabitants to pay them duty on their wine and salt trades. Later the Norwegian Vikings joined forces with Danes and embarked on expeditions to Spain and on into the Mediterranean.

The prime target for Norwegian expeditions were the British Isles. The Vikings penetrated southward from their newly founded colonies in the Shetlands, Faroes, Orkneys and Hebrides and settled in the north of Scotland, on the Isle of Man and along the north-west coast of England. Right up until the 18th century people in the Shetlands and Orkneys spoke Old Norse; the Faroes do so to the present day. Furthermore, many place-names witness to the Norwegian settlement of these districts.

The Danes, who had conquered a major part of England, and the Norwegians competed for control over York. For in Viking times York was one of the greatest trading places north of the Alps.

When Norwegians reached Ireland shortly after A.D.800, they met with little resistance. The island was divided into numerous, permanently warring small kingdoms. The Vikings established themselves along the coast, founded the first towns, introduced coinage and set in motion trade with the rest of Europe. Yet the Vikings' brutal behaviour caused the

Celtic population to unite against the attackers. The Irish were particularly provoked by Turgeis, the chief who founded Dublin. He wished to replace Christianity with the worship of Tor, god of thunder, and he built a heathen temple in Armagh, headquarters of the Christian Church in Ireland. Turgeis was captured and drowned by the Celts.

Before long the Celts learned from the Vikings how to build better ships and make better weapons. The Irish petty kings allied themselves with the Danes, and by about 900 the Norwegians had been driven out. But they returned. The last of the Norwegian Viking kingdoms in Ireland was crushed only as late as the beginning of the 11th century.

Some Vikings who strayed off course during a voyage from Norway to the British Isles in the second half of the 9th century discovered Iceland. It was already inhabited by Irish monks, but they left the island when the Vikings began settling there. Most of the new arrivals were from western Norway, many of them having sailed from Norway because they were unwilling to submit to King Harald Fairhair who was trying to unite the country. Many, too, came from the Norwegian settlements in Scotland and Ireland.

Around the year 930, Iceland was divided among some four hundred chiefs. They established an assembly of their own which they called the *Allting,* adopting laws of a Norwegian regional assembly (the *Gulating*). The slaves of Irish and Scottish descent who formed the majority of the population quickly had to abandon their Celtic culture.

Iceland became a centre of Old Norse saga literature. The sagas are a principal source for our knowledge of the Vikings and of medieval society. Although they were written down several hundred years after the events they describe took place, they contain a wealth of trustworthy information. The Sagas of the Kings are based on a number of heroic poems composed by the Viking kings' skalds or bards. The poems were in verse, and were preserved word for word as they were passed on from generation to generation until they were written down by Snorre Sturlason and other authors.

According to the sagas, the first Vikings settled on Greenland in the 980s. This colonising expedition was led by Eirik Raude of Rogaland in Norway, who had been outlawed after a murder on Iceland. He set off from there with 25 ships fully laden with people, cattle and equipment. Only 14 reached their destination. In the ensuing years over 250 farms were established in the Eastern Settlement and nearly 80 in the Western Settlement. These communities survived until c.1500, at which time the population died out, though the reason is not known.

In about the year 1000, Eirik's son Leiv led an expedition which followed the coast of North America. He spent a winter on the tip of Newfoundland at a place now called L'Anse aux Meadows. The area was given the name Vinland, most likely meaning «the land of beautiful grass». Several expeditions had Vinland as their goal, but no permanent habitation came into being there. Perhaps Indian attacks are the explanation.

The Unification of Norway

In 1904 a Viking ship was excavated in the county of Vestfold, the Oseberg ship. In it the archaeologists found grave goods unparalleled in Norway. The woman buried here had indeed had a sumptuous burial. No effort had been spared to make her journey to the kingdom of the dead a comfortable one. A maidservant had been sacrificed, as had several horses and dogs. In addition the ship contained kitchen and weaving utensils, a carriage, three sledges, chests, wall hangings, furniture, clothes, and agricultural implements. Many of these objects were finely carved, and they testify a luxury which must have belonged to the richest household in the country.

The sagas link Harald Fairhair with this family. Harald was eager to subdue the whole of Norway, though his motives in unifying the country have been obscured

Gold treasure from Hon in Eiker, Buskerud, late ninth century. The find included Arabic, Byzantine and Frankish coins and jewelry.

by time. Presumably, like most Vikings, he wished to increase his power and wealth.

It is reasonable to assume that the chiefs of Vestfold county obtained much of their income from the trading place Skiringssal. Perhaps they were responsible for its defence, and the merchants and craftsmen had to pay duties for this. However, the sea route along the Norwegian coast was fraught with danger: ships heading for Skiringssal from Trøndelag and the north of Norway were repeatedly attacked by Vikings of western Norway. It was probably in order to put an end to this piracy that Harald formed an alliance with the mighty earl of Lade in Trøndelag, who had important trading interests in the north. Together they waged war against the petty kings of western Norway. And at the end of the 9th century Harald won a decisive victory at Hafrsfjord in Rogaland.

Harald established no great system of

Accompanied by his bodyguard of warriors Harald travelled around the kingdom on royal progresses. Local farmers had to provide hospitality, both accommodation and food and beer, when the king and his retinue came to their district. Harald also stayed at his farms, many of them properties which had previously belonged to heads of households who were killed or who fled in the fighting as Norway was unified. To administer and police these royal farms Harald appointed bailiffs. They were responsible for law and order in the settlements, they punished wrongdoers, collecting fines from those who had broken the laws.

Harald had many sons, and when he died in c.930 the succession was bloodily contested. Håkon was victorious, and was acclaimed king by an assembly in Trøndelag. He promised to respect the laws and improve them, promises he in fact kept. He

«Leiv Eiriksson discovers America», Painting by Christian Krohg, 1903.

The beautiful, richly carved cart from the Oseberg find was probably used in religious and other processions.

is known as Håkon the Good.

With the cooperation of the farmers of western Norway and Trøndelag, Håkon established new regional assemblies (*lagting*). The deputies at the Gulating and the Frostating respectively were selected by the king's bailiffs, and the king attended sessions to discuss current matters. The assemblies passed judgements and formulated laws, and were presided over by a person particularly well versed in the laws, known as the *lagmann*. He recited the laws and interpreted them before the assembly made its decisions.

Håkon gained the agreement of the law assemblies to develop the system of naval levy called *leidang*. Laws ordained that the farmers were to man and equip longships for a period of two months. The ships were under the king's command, and were called up by means of signals from coastal beacons.

Both the assemblies and the naval defence measures strengthened the monarchy and the authority of the Hårfagr (Fairhair)

family, and yet there remained those who would not accept domination by one house over all others. After the death of Håkon the Good in 960, the earls of Lade in Trøndelag formed an alliance with Danish kings in a bid to gain control of the regions around the Oslo Fjord. This partnership in opposition to the Hårfagr attempt to rule Norway persisted until the 1030s.

Olav Tryggvason and Olav Haraldsson, both of the Hårfagr line, tried to secure the legacy of Håkon the Good. Both were great warriors who had amassed fortunes on Viking expeditions, particularly to England. They used their property and their gold for rewarding many retainers and buying the support of Norwegian heads of households. However, they faced formidable opposition. Olav Tryggvason was defeated after a mere five years: in 1000 he was killed at the Battle of Svolder.

During their expeditions in Europe the two Olavs had converted to Christianity, and on their return to Norway they tried to introduce Christianity by force. By the end of the 10th century the new faith had made progress in coastal areas, but many were against it, especially in inland parts of south-eastern Norway and in the north.

Several times a year great celebrations were held in honour of the gods. Leading men and women officiated at these sacrifices. It is likely that one of the women buried in the Oseberg ship was such a priestess of Frøya, goddess of fertility. The beautiful cart excavated in the mound could have served to move images or «priests» about the fields. Tapestry fragments from the same burial depict a scene which could be a procession of this kind. We also see a sacred grove, where human sacrifices hang from the trees. Ritual killings may have been performed in honour of Odin, the god of war.

These were the sort of customs Olav Haraldsson wished to put an end to when he arrived in Norway in 1015 to seize royal power. The timing was good. Olav's mightiest enemy, the king of Denmark, was busy with major campaigns in England, and so it was relatively easy for Olav to overcome the earls of Lade and establish a new realm.

Olav got several of the assemblies to pass laws which paved the way for Christianity. Buildings sacred to the old gods were pulled down, their images destroyed. To take their place he built churches and appointed priests, with himself as their head. People who continued to resist had to suffer death, or watch their farmsteads go up in flames.

Many heads of households feared that Christianity would deprive them of their positions as religious leaders. For their sacerdotal function was closely linked to their status at the assemblies and in battle. It therefore comes as no surprise that Olav acquired many enemies around Lake Mjøsa and in Trøndelag, districts where the old religion was most deeply entrenched.

Olav needed to win the most powerful families in the country over to his side. He allowed them to keep the income from their farms and to take over duties from

the bailiffs. In return they had to swear allegiance to him.

However, the majority of household heads were not satisfied with the prestige offered by this position of vassal. Even though many of them had become Christians, they feared that Olav's power over them would be too great. And so it was not difficult for Knut (Canute) the Great, King of Denmark, to gain the support of disaffected Norwegian household heads when he in 1025 decided to incorporate Norway into his North Sea empire. Generous gifts of money from his treasury tempted many.

Olav had to flee the country, but came back to fight. In 1030 he faced his opponents at Stiklestad in Trøndelag. This is how Snorre describes the crucial moments: *«Thorstein the Shipwright struck with his axe at King Olav, and the blow fell on his left leg above the knee. After that wound the King leaned up against a stone, cast away his sword and bade God help him. Then Tore the Hound struck at him with his spear, and the thrust went up under the brynie up into his stomach. Kalv then struck him, and the blow fell on the left side of his neck. ... These three wounds brought about King Olav's fall.»*

To all appearances, the Hårfagr family had lost the struggle for royal power in Norway.

The Fall of King Olav Haraldsson at Stiklestad, drawing by Erik Werenskiold in Snorre's Sagas of the Kings.

The Viking Age

The period from the end of the 8th century to the mid 11th century in Scandinavia is known as the Viking Age. Over the preceding century the population had increased rapidly, and in western Norway all the arable land was under cultivation. Ground was cleared for new farms inland, but that was not sufficient. And so, skilful shipbuilders as they were and armed with good weapons of iron, many set off overseas in search of land and wealth. Soon the warriors from Scandinavia were feared far and wide in Europe.

Those who went on the voyages were called «Vikings». Danes and Norwegians tended to head westward, to islands in the Atlantic and to the Frankish

On the band above the map is shown the alphabet used by the Vikings. These symbols are known as runes.

Vikings in the west

Eirik Raude's son Leiv was the first European to reach the coast of North America. He called the land he came to Vinland. People on Greenland needed timber, and this may have been why they sought new land to the west. In the 1960s Norwegian archaeologists found the remains of a Viking settlement at L'Anse aux Meadows on Newfoundland. The settlers abandoned Vinland after a time, presumably because they were attacked by Indians.

On the band below is a runic inscription of c.1020 from Galteland in Evje in the Setesdal valley. *«Arnstein raised this stone for Bjor his son. He met his death in battle when Knut attacked England.»*

Colonisation of Iceland began in the 870s. Chief Eirik Raude sailed further westward, and around the year 985 he discovered a new land he named Greenland.

GRØNLAND

Vestribygd

Austribygd

Brattalid

MARKLAND

• L'Anse aux Meadows

VINLAND

(Newfoundland)

A reconstruction drawing of the Viking farmstead Jarlshof on Shetland. The island was only a day's voyage from Norway. The houses were built of stone, earth and turf.

The excavations at L'Anse aux Meadows were conducted by Helge and Anne Stine Ingstad. Leiv Eiriksson's house may have looked like this.

Empire, while Swedes sailed east to Russia. At this time Scandinavia really became a part of Europe.

The Vikings were expert warriors who sacked and pillaged. They took prisoners and sold them as slaves. But they were also efficient merchants, craftsmen and farmers who established new states. Norwegian Vikings settled first in the Shetlands, Orkneys, Hebrides and Faroes. Later they colonised parts of Scotland and northern England, the Isle of Man, Ireland, Iceland and Greenland. They also reached the coast of Newfoundland. Moreover Norwegian and Danish Vikings went on expeditions to the Frankish Empire to trade and plunder; there they were known as the Northmen. Led by the chief Rollo they founded a Viking state in Normandy. Rollo became a duke recognised by the French king, and Normandy became an important centre of power and influence in 11th-century Europe.

The Vikings brought Christianity back with them to Scandinavia. Administrative concepts gleaned in continental Europe played an important role in the evolution of the Norwegian monarchy in the Middle Ages.

The largest and most important Viking town in England was Jorvik (York). Norwegian and Danish chiefs fought for supremacy in the town, and against the inhabitants they found there.

York now has an impressive Viking museum illustrating life in the town's homes, workshops and streets over a thousand years ago. Several street names in York derive from Viking days.

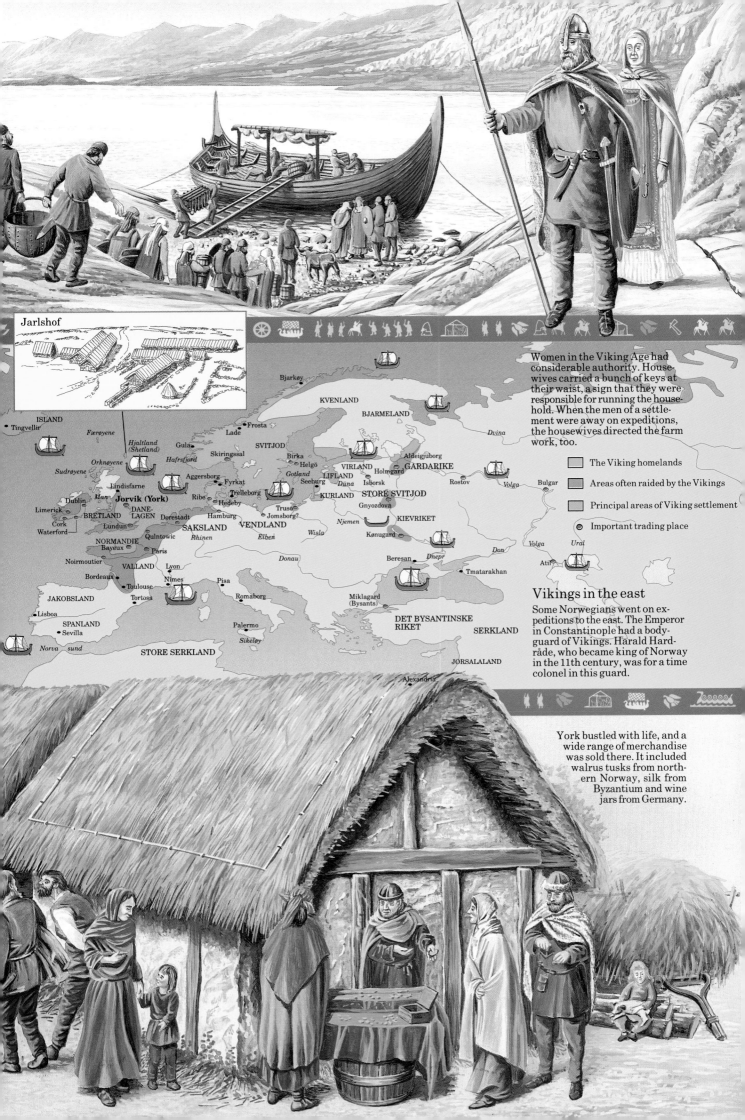

Jarlshof

Women in the Viking Age had considerable authority. Housewives carried a bunch of keys at their waist, a sign that they were responsible for running the household. When the men of a settlement were away on expeditions, the housewives directed the farm work, too.

The Viking homelands

Areas often raided by the Vikings

Principal areas of Viking settlement

● Important trading place

Vikings in the east

Some Norwegians went on expeditions to the east. The Emperor in Constantinople had a bodyguard of Vikings. Harald Hardråde, who became king of Norway in the 11th century, was for a time colonel in this guard.

York bustled with life, and a wide range of merchandise was sold there. It included walrus tusks from northern Norway, silk from Byzantium and wine jars from Germany.

ISLAND
Tingvellir
Færøyene
Hjaltland (Shetland)
Orknøyene
Sudrøyene
Lindisfarne
Man
Dublin
Limerick
Cork
Waterford
BRETLAND
DANELAGEN
Jorvik (York)
Lundun
Dorestadt
NORMANDIE
Bayeux
Noirmoutier
Bordeaux
Toulouse
Tortosa
JAKOBSLAND
Lisboa
SPANLAND
Sevilla
Norva sund
STORE SERKLAND
Qulntowic
Rhinen
Paris
Lyon
VALLAND
Nîmes
Pisa
Romaborg
Palermo
Sikeløy
Bjarkøy
KVENLAND
BJARMELAND
Dvina
Lade
Frosta
Gula
Skiringssal
SVITJOD
Birka
Helgö
Gotland
Seeburg
LIFLAND
Düna
KURLAND
Fyrkat
Trelleborg
Ribe
Hedeby
Hamburg
Jomsborg?
Truso
SAKSLAND
VENDLAND
Elben
Wisla
Njemen
KIEVRIKET
Kønugard
Donau
Beresan
Dnepr
Miklagard (Bysants)
DET BYSANTINSKE RIKET
JORSALALAND
Alexandria
VIRLAND
Holmgard
Aldeigjuborg
GARDARIKE
Isborsk
STORE SVITJOD
Gnyozdova
Rostov
Volga
Bulgar
Don
Volga
Ural
Atil
SERKLAND
Aggersborg
Hafrsfjord

THE MIDDLE AGES 1030-1537

King and Church in the Century of Peace 1030–1130

Pray to Olav
that he may grant you
power in his country,
he is a man of God;
he can obtain
from God Himself
years and peace
for all men.

These words were recited by the scald, Torarin Lovtunge, to Svein Alfivason, who was crowned King of Norway after the fall of King Olav Haraldson. Svein was a son of the Danish king and since he was only ten years old, his mother came with him to help him govern. Danish rule was soon regarded as a burden. New taxes were levied on peasant families and bad harvests reduced many to eating bark bread. Svein's reputation suffered accordingly. An unlucky ruler could be a disaster for the country. Torarin had good reason for recommending Svein to seek help from Olav, the man of God.

Svein's rule was also challenged by Olav himself. A group of farmers had carried his body away after the battle of Stiklestad and had buried it in the sand by the Nid

The Life and Death of Saint Olav, communion table, probably from Haltdalen stave church in Trøndelag, c. 1300. Today it is in Nidaros Cathedral, Trondheim.

Opposite page: Heddal Church was built in about 1250 and is the biggest stave church in Norway.

Madonna and child from Enebakk Church in Akershus.

scendants claimed a special right to the throne of Norway. Olav had become *rex perpetuus Norvegiae* – «Eternal King of Norway».

The royal saint became a symbol of unity and the King's enemies accepted the fact that his power continued after his death. The Danes soon had to leave and Olav's son, Magnus, was brought home from Russia to be the new King. The century after the Battle of Stiklestad is rightly called the «Century of Peace». Peace reigned until the death of King Sigurd Jorsalfar in 1130. The country entered into a period of growth and prosperity and the first cities were founded.

After 1030, everyone accepted centralised royal authority. During the Viking Age many people in rural areas had been on the move and many of the overlords had absed their power. The ordinary farmers probably felt that the King's men would protect them. The King was regarded as a peacemaker. Danish rule after 1030 also taught Norwegians that the country could be threatened from the outside and although it would be incorrect to speak of national unity in the Century of Peace, people from Trøndelag and Vestfold probably felt that they had more in common with each other than with the Danes.

After the country's conversion to Christianity, the clergy presented the relationship between God and man in a simple way. The battle stood between Satan, who ruled in Hell, and Christ, who was the key to salvation and eternal life with God in Heaven. The Lord Jesus stood at the head of a host of angels. People had to choose the right side and the saints took over the role of helpers of the people that had previously been filled by the heathen gods. Saint Olav was now the one who warded off trolls and the power of evil, a role previously held by Thor. Saint Nicholas took over from Frøy as the protector of fertility. His name lives on in the Norwegian word *nisse*.

The King was head of the Norwegian Church in the Century of Peace. Norway did not become a separate archdiocese

river. Many rumours were soon circulating about miracles that had taken place close to the King's grave. The bishop to Olav's *hird* went north to Nidaros and one year after the King's death the body was disinterred in the presence of the country's most prominent people. According to legend, Olav was as handsome as the day he was buried and his beard and hair had continued to grow. The body was laid in a casket and placed in St. Clement's Church and Saint Olav was canonised by the bishop. This is how the kings of Norway came to have direct ties to God through their saintly predecessor, and Olav's de-with its own archbishop at Nidaros until 1152. The Church needed the authority of the King to ensure the country's conversion to Christianity. The King needed the well-organised administrative system of the Church, and the Church upheld the King's claim to have received his power from God. When a priest was to be appointed, the farmers proposed a candidate to the bishop and he usually followed their advice. The farmers paid the priests themselves and the maintenance of the parish church was a communal responsibility. Thus the Norwegian Church became not only the church of the King but also the church of the people during the Century of Peace. The Norwegians were keen church builders, too. Norwegian lords and freeholders built 800 churches in the Middle Ages, most of which were wooden stave churches.

By the mid 1100s the power of the King and the authority of the Church were undisputed in Norway. But now that the King and the Church were in a position to enforce their demands and impositions, somebody had to pay. This is the background to be kept in mind when we turn to developments in rural society in the Middle Ages.

Rural Society in the Middle Ages

Between 1000 and 1300, the Norwegian population increased from 150,000 to about 400,000 and new land was brought under the plough all over the country. A total of 5,000 farms were cleared in the South-East, as can be seen from the large number of names ending in -rud (clearing). The increase in population also led to the partitioning of farmlands. This was particularly the case in the West, where there was little land available.

The farmers had owned their own farms in the Viking Age, but 300 years later much of the land had changed ownership. The majority of farmers were tenants under the King, the Church or the overlords, who together owned about 70 per cent of the land. Strong forces had led to

this change in ownership. During the unification of Norway, the kings confiscated the land of any farmers who defied them. The kings also demanded the right to any untitled lands; all those who cleared new farms therefore automatically became tenants of the king. In the 12th and 13th centuries the population increased and when there was a bad harvest, farmers had to borrow from the king, the Church or the overlords. If they could not repay their debts the creditor acquired the rights to all or part of the farm. The farmer continued to work the land, but now as a tenant. It was also customary for people from all

Crucifix from Horg Church in North Trøndelag, showing Christ with a royal crown.

social strata to donate land to the Church so that the priests would pray for them. These gifts contributed towards making the Church Norway's biggest landowner.

Norwegian farmers were nevertheless freer than farmers living on large estates elsewhere in Europe. The Norwegian landowners owned only individual farms which lay miles apart, or they might own only parts of farms. The country was large and rugged and the farmers seldom saw the landowner. Norwegian farmers were legally free throughout the Middle Ages.

The labour of the farmers and their families supported the upper classes. They paid rents to the landowners, taxes to the King and tithes to the Church. The farmers were responsible for maintaining the churches and providing transport for the King's men who travelled through their area. Both King and Church had the right to collect fines from lawbreakers. The average farmer in the 13th century paid about 20 per cent of his family's production to the King, the Church and the overlords.

The Civil War Period 1130–1217

In the 1120s the Irishman Gilchrist («Servant of God») came to Norway and demanded to be King. To prove that he was the son of King Magnus Berrføtt (Barefoot) he walked over nine red-hot ploughshares and the saga relates that his feet bore no signs of burns three days later. Sigurd Jorsalfar (so-called because of his visit to Jerusalem) was King at the time. He accepted the event as a clear sign from God but Gilchrist promised not to allow himself to be acclaimed King until Sigurd himself and his son, Magnus, were dead. This agreement was of little value. When Sigurd died in 1130 not only Magnus was acclaimed but also Magnus and Gilchrist, who now called himself Harald Gille. Harald had Magnus maimed and killed but was later murdered by a new pretender. The Civil War in Norway had begun. The century of civil war should not be overdramatised, however. The population increased rapidly, new land was cleared, the revenues of the King and the Church increased and there were long periods of peace.

One of the reasons for the outbreak of civil war in Norway was the system of royal succession. All the king's sons, whether legitimate or illegitimate, had the right to become king and ruled together in a «joint monarchy». Thanks to unbelievable luck, there had been no internal strife in Norway during the Century of Peace. After 1130, the pretenders to the throne were often small children. Behind them were powerful lords with supporters in various parts of the country who were interested in promoting their own interests. This was another important contributory factor to the civil war.

The power of the Church increased during the tumultuous civil war period. The demand for freedom of the Church from temporal control had also reached Norway. With the establishment of the Archbishopric of Nidaros in 1152, the Norwegian Church had its own leader and under Archbishop Øystein (1161–1188) it attempted to form a kingdom which it would be able to influence and control. The Archbishop supported Erling Skakke, who was married to the daughter of Sigurd

Thirteenth century battle scene. Carving on a chair from Blakar Farm, Lom, Gudbrandsdalen.

Jorsalfar. Their son, Magnus, was a legitimate child of this marriage. Magnus had no legal right of accession to the throne but the Church wanted him on the throne because he was legitimate. Erling Skakke saw an opportunity for political gain and defeated the other pretenders. In 1163 the Archbishop crowned and blessed seven-year-old Magnus Erlingsson King of Norway. At the same time, a law was passed forbidding joint monarchy and awarding the right of succession to the King's oldest legitimate son. The King was to be elected by 60 farmers from all over the country but their choice could be rejected by the bishops if they considered the chosen one to be unsuited for royal power. The events of 1163 were a victory for the Church and for Erling Skakke.

Erling and Magnus were not left in peace, however. They were continually fighting potential pretenders to the throne. In 1177 a man called Sverre landed in Norway. He had grown up in the Faroes and studied for the priesthood, and he maintained that he was the son of a king. Most historians agree that he could not have been a king's son, but it is possible that he believed it himself. Sverre became the leader of a group of rebels called the «Birkebeiners». This nickname was due to the fact that they were so poor that they could not afford proper shoes and instead wore shoes made of birch bark.

Sverre and his men were supported by many of Erling Skakke's enemies. Erling was killed in 1179 and King Magnus died five years later. But Sverre was still not the supreme ruler and the strongest opposition came from the Church. In the 1190s the Church and a number of lords created the «Bagler Party». Sverre was excommunicated and remained so until his death in 1202.

His son, Håkon, managed to reach an agreement with the Church, and Sverre's descendants and the Church leaders gradually became reconciled. The King of the Birkebeiners and the King of the Baglers nevertheless each ruled their own regions until 1217, when both died. Thirteen-year-

old Håkon Håkonsson was now elected King. His mother, Inga of Varteig, vouched for his being the illegitimate grandson of King Sverre. The following year she carried glowing iron seven paces to prove her son's high birth and that she had God on her side, just as Gilchrist had done a century before. Young Håkon ruled alone.

Norway's Golden Age

Thirty years were to pass before the Pope would bless the illegitimate king and even then it was at a price. The Pope was paid a large sum of money to agree to disregard the fact that Håkon was illegitimate and promise that the King's descendants should succeed him. This is the origin of the Norwegian hereditary monarchy.

In June 1247, Cardinal William of Sabina

Most people lived in open-hearth huts in the Middle Ages. The hearth was in the middle of the room and the smoke went out through a hole in the roof. This open-hearth hut from Tolstad in Vågå stands today at Maihaugen, Lillehammer.

came to Bergen as representative of the Pope. Håkon was crowned in the Church of Christ on 29 July, the anniversary of Saint Olav's death. The coronation showed that Håkon Håkonsson used foreign courts as his model and that the ceremonies and celebrations followed European custom. Perhaps it is nationalistic boasting to label the thirteenth century as «Norway's Golden Age». The country was almost entirely a rural society and the Norwegian state was poor compared with most others. All the same, the thirteenth century was the period when Norway gained a place among the kingdoms of Europe.

During the Golden Age, the kings of Norway controlled more territory than ever before. England was the country's main trading partner and Norwegian longships carried salt herring, dried fish and wood products to English ports. The return cargo was mainly corn, but also included woollen cloth, weapons and luxury goods.

Trade in the thirteenth century increased cultural influences from the West and the South. In England and France. Norwegian artisans learned to build churches and the castles that were built were based on French designs. Akershus Castle in Oslo and Vardøhus Castle in Finnmark are typical examples. French romances and stories from the Orient were read aloud at the Norwegian court and gradually spread to the rest of the population. The foreign influences mingled with Norwegian traditions and the country developed its own folk lore during the Middle Ages. People sang and danced to the folk songs, and folk stories were passed on from one generation to the next in the centuries that followed. The Norwegian controlled lands produced great authors, too. The most prominent of these was the Icelander Snorre Sturlason, who wrote the sagas of the Norwegian kings up to the time of King Sverre. This great work is our primary source of knowledge of early Norwegian history.

Towards the end of the 1200s the

Germans took over as Norway's most important trading partners. The population increased rapidly and the country did not have enough corn. The German Baltic cities did, however, and the Hanseatic merchant ships were better suited to carrying corn than the old Norwegian longships. In the 1300s the King was forced to give the cities of Lübeck, Bremen and other members of the Hanseatic League preferential rights over Norwegian merchants. Bergen was the most important city during the Golden Age and a community of German merchants and artisans was established there.

The power of the king increased during the Golden Age. The country was divided into 50 districts (*sysler*) and the district governors (*sysselmenn*) and their subordinates collected taxes and organised conscription. Although the central administration was extremely limited, the Royal Chancellor played a key role. He held the royal seal and corresponded in the name of the King with many people at home and abroad. The King held supreme power but did not decide everything alone. In order to ensure that his decisions were effective and because he required help, he was advised by his lords and bishops. From the 1280s these «good men» functioned as a permanent royal council. It was essential to have the bishops on this council. The King needed the leaders of the Church because he maintained that his power came from God. They knew Latin and had theological and legal training. At the same time, the Church needed the power of the King to protect its own interests.

The King increased his control of the legal system. King Magnus Lagabøte (Law-Mender) caused a new law to be written for the whole country, based on the old laws laid down by the five ancient *lagting*. The national law was passed by each individual *lagting*. This shows that the King still had respect for the farmers on the council, but in reality legal authority came under royal control. The King now appointed his own presiding judges (*lagmenn*), who became the *de facto* judges.

Opposite page:
Håkon Håkonsson was crowned in the Church of Christ, Bergen, on 29 July 1247. Gerhard Munthe's impression of the coronation ceremony can be seen in this tapestry of 1910.

Finally, the King forbade blood feud. The state would now be reponsible for punishing criminals.

The old Norwegian state was based on insecure foundations, however. Håkon Håkonsson's Law of Succession of 1260 laid down that the King's oldest legitimate son should inherit the throne after his father. Håkon V Magnusson, who reigned at the beginning of the fourteenth century, did not have a son and his daughter, Ingebjørg, married a Swedish duke. She gave birth to his son, Magnus. In spring 1319 the country's most prominent men swore at Håkon V Magnussons's deathbed that no foreigner should own a castle or fiefdom in Norway and that the country should be free. The dying king sensed the threat to come.

Håkonshallen in Bergen was finished in time for the coronation of Magnus Lagabøte (Lawmender) in 1261. The King's throne stands at the end of the hall, as it did in the Middle Ages.

Union and Depopulation in the Late Middle Ages 1319–1537

When Håkon V died, three-year-old Magnus succeeded to the Norwegian throne. He was elected King of Sweden in the same year and the two kingdoms therefore became a personal union. In Norway the King's Council, which was now known as the *Council of the Realm,* was to govern under the Queen Mother, Ingebjørg, until Magnus came of age. However, both Ingebjørg and Magnus came into conflict with the Council. When Ingebjørg tried to take over the Danish province of Skåne, the Council expelled her from the government. Magnus continued to follow Ingebjørg's policies from the time he came of age until he was deposed in 1343.

The Swedish and Norwegian Councils of the Realm forced the King to accept the proposal that his two sons should inherit one country each as soon as they came of age. The Council of the Realm was trying to repair the damage that had been done by joint rule. But Norway was soon to be affected by a greater disaster. In the summer of 1349 the plague came to Bergen, carried by an English ship.

The plague spread rapidly. During that autumn and winter, one third of the population was wiped out by the Black Death. There were other, smaller epidemics in the following decades and by 1400 the population had been halved compared with the Golden Age. What were the consequences for Norway of this enormous loss?

The plague disasters led to an improvement in the lives of ordinary people. After 1350, the farmers that survived were able to take over the best land. Whole communities had been wiped out and people moved from the smaller farms. The reclamation of these farms did not begin until the 16th century and the bad times live on in local names, such as Ødegård and Aunli (deserted farm). It also became cheaper to rent land and the farmers paid less in taxes and tithes. In 1500 taxation was half what it had been in the Golden Age. The lack of manpower led many to change from corn to cattle farming and the nation's diet contained more protein than before.

The State did not fare so well. The loss of income weakened the power of the King. In rural areas the peasants took over many of the responsibilities themselves. The legal system is one example. The old *bygdeting,* where the farmers passed judgement in private court cases, flourished again.

The nobility was also weaker. The lesser nobility joined the ranks of the farmers because their land produced less income than before. The higher nobility, who held the King's fief, did better. Weaker royal power gave the overlords more room for manoeuvre. Compared with the nobility in neighbouring countries, however, the Norwegian lords were few and impoverished, and Swedes and Danes were soon

marrying into the Norwegian aristocracy.

The Church did better. Although its income was also affected, it was the biggest landowner in the country. In the late Middle Ages people feared death more than ever and attempted to save their souls by donating land to the Church. The Archbishop of Nidaros became the most powerful man in Norway and was the uncontested leader of the Council of the Realm. Most of his tithes were paid in dried fish, which he sold to the Hanseatic merchants in Bergen. Would the leaders of the Church and the weakened nobility be able to preserve the independence of the Norwegian State?

Norway was inferior to Sweden and Denmark. Their populations were larger and their arable land much more extensive. In the 14th and 15th centuries, the Hanseatic League took control of Norwegian foreign trade and there was growing apprehension in Scandinavia about the economic and political advances of the

According to popular tradition, the plague was an old woman called «Pesta». If she used her broom, everyone in her way was doomed to die. If she used her rake, some people survived. Painting by Th. Kittelsen, 1904.

Painting of 1885 by Vilhelm Rosenstand showing King Christian II and his mistress, the beautiful Dyveke from Bergen.

Germans. This is the background for the Union of Kalmar (1389–1521).

Margrete was a Danish princess who became Queen of Norway when she married Håkon VI Magnusson. She survived her father, her husband and her son and managed to get her young relation, Eric of Pomerania, elected King of both Norway and Denmark. She then attacked Sweden, where the nobility were discontented with their German king. He was exiled and Eric was crowned King of Scandinavia in the town of Kalmar in 1397. Margrete ruled all three kingdoms with a firm hand.

Her policies were intended to strengthen royal power and weaken the Councils of the Realm. Sweden and Norway were to be subject to the main country, Denmark. In Norway no full sessions of the Council of the Realm were summoned and the Seal of the Realm, the symbol of sovereignty,

was taken to Copenhagen, where the King of the Union resided. The Queen was supported by Norwegian lords and bishops. Eric of Pomerania continued Margrete's anti-German policies, which led to wars with both German princes and the Hanseatic League. Bergen was attacked and plundered and German ships crushed the Norwegian conscript fleet. German blockade and heavy taxation affected Norway deeply. The farmers rebelled, both in Norway and Sweden, and the Swedish nobility managed to withdraw their country from the union. The Norwegian Council of the Realm was too weak, however. It was impossible to re-create a separate Norwegian kingdom.

Christian II became King of Denmark and Norway in 1513. The Norwegian Council of the Realm was ignored, the King made his non-aristocratic supporters into overlords and his private secretary became Archbishop of Nidaros. Christian wanted to restore the Union of Kalmar and conquered Sweden, but this was the beginning of the end. After his coronation in Stockholm in 1520, he had 82 nobles and clergy murdered in an attempt to frighten others into submission. The Swedish and Danish nobility rose against «Christian the Tyrant» and in 1523 he fled to the Netherlands.

Norway stayed in the background during this struggle but a powerful politician, Olav Engelbrektsson, now took over the Archbishop's throne in Nidaros. The teachings of Martin Luther were well known in Denmark and the Archbishop realised that they might soon be a threat to the Catholic Church in Norway. As leader of the Council of the Realm, he made every effort to keep the country free of the «Lutheran poison» but he was unsuccessful. An alliance with the German Kaiser and the exiled Christian II failed. The Archbishop's uprising ended in total defeat. In 1537, King Christian III's forces reached Norway. The new King was a Lutheran who had introduced the Reformation into Denmark the previous year. He now demanded the Norwegian throne.

The Kingdom of Norway is Crushed

On Easter Sunday, 1 April 1537, Olav Engelbrektsson sailed down the Trondheim fjord on his way to the Netherlands. Norway's last Archbishop had lost the battle for the Catholic Church and for the independence of the Norwegian state. As he saw the country vanish on the horizon he must have reflected on what had gone wrong. The plague and depopulation had been a disaster for both Church and state, and the neighbouring countries had been stronger in the period of union. Perhaps the most bitter blow was Christian III's betrayal of the true Church, so that he, the Primate of the Church and Head of the Council of the Realm, had to flee the country. The joyful message of the Easter celebrations could hardly have been enough to assuage Olav's grief. He died in the Netherlands in the following year, by which time King Christian III had a strong hold on the realm and the church, a hold which his successors were to maintain for another 280 years.

Queen Margrete's sarcophagus in Roskilde Cathedral, Denmark.

The Middle Ages

After the fall of the saintly King Olav in 1030, the Norwegian population increased, reaching about 400,000 the mid-1300s. The king gained control of the whole country in the eleventh century and the first towns appeared. Norway was converted to Christianity and controlled by the Church, the king and the overlords. There was widespread unrest in the twelfth century and the period from 1130 to 1217 is known as the Civil War Period. Pretenders to the throne fought to win the kingdom. The thirteenth century is often called the «Golden Age». At this time the King of Norway controlled more territory than in any other period. In 1349 the country was ravaged by a plague known as the «Black Death» and about one third of the population died.

GRØNLAND 1261 - 1814

Vestribygd

Eystribygd

Gardar

In this drawing by Erik Werenskiold we see bishops and overlords paying homage to Magnus Erlingsson after his coronation in 1163. This was the first coronation in Scandinavia.

The child-king Magnus needed the support of the Church because he was not a king's son. He was killed by Sverre Sigurdsson, another pretender to the throne, when he was only twenty-seven years old.

This drawing shows life on a farm in the Middle Ages. The farmers had to give one fifth of their production to the king, the Church and the overlords. The Church owned about 40 percent of the land and was the biggest landowner in the country.

The Baldishol tapestry from Nes in Hedmark county may have been woven as early as the 13th century. The knight with his lance and shield is thought to symbolise the month of May. Although knights such as this were common in the rest of Europe, there were few of them in Norway.

Gol Stave Church, dating from the thirteenth century, is one of approximately 800 wooden churches that were built by farmers in the Middle Ages. Today it stands in the Norwegian Folk Museum in Oslo.

Håkonshallen in Bergen was built by King Håkon Håkonsson and was completed in 1261 in time for the wedding of his son, Magnus, to Ingebjørg, daughter of the Danish King, Erik Plogpenning.

Bergen was the largest and most important town in the Middle Ages. A community of German craftsmen and merchants grew up on the quayside. Bryggens Museum and the Hanseatic Museum in Bergen provide a lively impression of town life and trade.

King Magnus Lagabøte (law-mender) established a common law for the whole country in the 1270s. The illustration shows part of the first page of the book of laws. The King is giving the law to a representative of the people.

ISLAND 1262 - 1814

Hólar

Skálholt

  Area of Norwegian sovereignty and the Archdiocese of Norway
● Town
⚓ Archbishopric
✝ Bishopric
■ Regional assembly (ting)
○ Other important trading posts

The most important exports were hides, furs, down, dried fish and timber. The main imports were corn, salt and malt but imports also included textiles and luxury goods.

From about 1100 until the 1260s the Isle of Man and the Hebrides were under Norwegian sovereignty. In 1266 these islands were ceded to the King of Scotland. The Orkney and Shetland Islands were pawned to another Scottish king as security for a dowry in the mid 1400s. Iceland, Greenland and the Faroes belonged to Norway and later to Denmark-Norway until 1814.

Kirkjubær
FÆRØYENE TIL 1814
Hjaltland
JARLEDØMMET ORKNØYENE
Orknøyene
Kirkjuvagr
SUDRØYENE
SUDRØYENE OG MAN BISPEDØMME
Perth
SKOTTLAND

IRLAND
Dublin
Peel
Isle of Man

NORDSJØEN

Vardøhus

Vågan
Trondenes
Steigo

NIDARÅS BISPEDØMME

Steinkjer
Nidaros
Veøy
Frøson
Borgund

JAMTALAND (under Uppsala bispedømme)

BOTTEN-VIKA

SVERIGE

Gävle
Åland
Viborg
Borgå
Åbo

BJØRGVIN BISPEDØMME
Bjørgvin
Lusakaupang
Lillehammer
HAMAR BISPEDØMME
Hamar

OSLO BISPEDØMME
Oslo
Hedemora
Örebro
Öregrund
Uppsala
Västerås
Stockholm

Stavanger
STAVANGER BISPEDØMME
Tønsberg
Skien
Borg
Tingvalla
Skara
Vadstena

NOVGOROD-RIKET

Dagö
Reval
Narva
ESTLAND
Hapsal
Pernau
Dorpat
Ösel

Gotland
Vishy

DEN TYSKE ORDENSSTAT
Riga

ØSTER-SJØEN

SAMOGITIA

Marstrand
Konghelle

DANMARK
Randers
Århus
Kolding
Flensburg
Kiel

Växjö
Kalmar
Öland

Helsingør
Hälsingborg
København
Lund
Malmö
Nyborg
Nykøbing
Rønne
Bornholm

Rügenswalde
Kolberg
Wollin
Golinow
Danzig
Elbing
Königsberg
Memel

LITAUEN
Minsk

DEN TYSKE ORDENSSTAT
Kulm

POLEN
Gniezno

Scarborough
Hull
Grimsby
Boston
Nottingham
Lynn

WALES

ENGLAND

London

Stralsund
Rostock
Wismar
Lübeck
Hamburg
Bremen
Emden
Groningen

DET TYSK-ROMERSKE RIKE

Harderwijk
Arnhem
Braunschweig
Magdeburg

Isle of Wight

Jersey

Brugge
Köln
Lüttich
Dinant

VOLHYNIA

Around 1300 most of the land was farmed by tenant farmers. The tenants were free, but they had to pay rent to the landowner. They paid in corn, butter, furs, hides and fish and also had to to maintain the farm buildings. A farm usually had several owners and the man who farmed the land was often one of them. The typical Norwegian farmer was therefore both a tenant and a freeholder. Norway did not have large estates or manors like those found in other European countries in the Middle Ages.

Rouen
FRANKRIKE
Paris
BRETAGNE
Nantes
Brest

Lyon

Bordeaux

AKVITANIA
Bayonne

The Hanseatic League.
The Hanseatic towns dominated foreign trade.
■ The most important towns
● Other important Hanseatic towns

Male dress of about 1500, giving an idea of clothing styles in the late Middle Ages.

Valence

NAVARRA
TILIEN
ARAGONIEN

Arles
Marseille
Toulon
Nice
Pisa
Firenze
Mantua
Genova
Bologna
Ravenna
Venezia
Trieste

VENEZIA
KROATIA
KIRKE-STATEN
BOSNIA
UNGARN
SERBIA
VALAKIA

GALICJA
Lwow

0   100   200 km

NORWAY IN UNION WITH DENMARK 1537-1814

·ADORNATA·FVIT·CONSILIO·D·IOANNIS·IACOBI·PASTORIS·HVIVS·ECCLESIÆ·ANNO·DNI

«Under the Danish Crown for Time Everlasting»

Norway's fate was formally sealed in 1536. In the autumn of that year Christian III and his lancers had conquered Denmark and introduced the Reformation. The accession charter stated:

«that the realm of Norway (.....) shall (.......) hereafter be and remain under the Danish crown just as any of the other lands, Jutland, Fyn or Skåne, and hereafter neither be nor be called a separate kingdom, but a part of the realm of Denmark and under the Danish crown for time everlasting».

King Christian and the Danish nobility had determined that Norway should cease to be an independent kingdom without the consent of a single Norwegian. The Norwegian Council of the Realm was gone for ever. After the defeat of the Catholic Church, the small Norwegian aristocracy was too weak to uphold the independence of the realm. From now on Norway was governed from Copenhagen, where power was divided between the King and his council of nobles. When one king died, a new king was elected by the Council of the Realm. He automatically also became King of Norway.

The Norwegian Nation Lives On

Norway never became a part of Denmark, as laid down in the coronation charter, because the ties binding people and country were too strong. Although Danish became the written language, Norwegian dialects and customs lived on. The Norwegians were conscious of being Norwegian and the kings called themselves King of Denmark and Norway. Coins that were minted in Norway bore the Norwegian coat of arms and the Danes themselves were never in any doubt that Norway was a separate realm. The section concerning Norway in King Christian III's coronation

Lutheran service in 1561, Torslunde Church, Denmark.

Opposite page: C. A. Lorentzen: «The Sarp Waterfall in Øst-fold», c. 1790.

This reliquary from the Church of St. Thomas in Fillefjell was probably made in Bergen in the thirteenth century. Historians believe it is similar to the reliquary of St. Olav which stood i Nidaros Cathedral.

charter was therefore only a paper provision. Norway lived on as a separate nation.

Norway experienced a period of rich growth in the centuries that followed. The population increased rapidly. Norwegian goods were in demand and fish, wood and minerals were the main Norwegian exports. However, Norway was primarily a country of farmers during the union period and the rural population lived frugally. The independence of the Norwegian state meant less to them than the struggle for their daily bread.

Norway, the Reformation and the Power of the King, 1537–1660

The Reformation strengthened the power of the king. The king in Copenhagen was now head of the Church instead of the Pope in Rome. There had been no Lutheran movement as there had been in Denmark and the Norwegians were forced to adopt the new faith. It must have seemed strange when saints, relics and monasteries disappeared, and the Danish sermon had an important place in the new church services.

It took time to find qualified ministers, however, and many of those who were chosen in the first decades after the Reformation were ignorant, quarrelsome drunkards. Nevertheless the ministers gradually became a useful tool for the state. They could preach the king's case «to the simple, ignorant, common people».

There was also an economic side to the Reformation. Prior to 1537 the Catholic Church was the largest landowner, owning over 40 per cent of the land. All this was now the property of the King.

The king increased his power in other areas too. Norway was divided into five main fiefdoms and a number of smaller ones. The Norwegian fiefdoms were granted by the king, mainly to Danish noblemen. At the beginning of the period, the overlord was responsible for most of the administration, but the king gradually increased his powers at the expense of the overlords. Historians speak of a transition from government by overlords to the government by royal officials in the century prior to 1660. From the end of the 1500s the overlords had to present proper accounts. In reality they were put on a fixed salary. The bailiff, who had originally been the personal servant of the overlord, became a royal official. It was the bailiffs who collected taxes and were responsible for law and order in their bailiwicks, and it was important that the king should control those who faced his subjects on a daily basis.

Society became increasingly complicated in the century after 1536. The need for specialised knowledge increased.It had been one of the responsibilities of the overlord to lead his troops into battle, but from the 1620s the king employed professional officers. This is how professional soldiers came to lead the Norwegian farmer army.

We therefore find stronger royal power and a weakened nobility in the first half of the 17th century. Many people see Christian IV (1588–1648) as the most influential of the kings who reigned in the century after the Reformation. He was «the King who discovered Norway». He had great hopes for the opportunities that lay waiting to be exploited in the Norwegian forests and mountains and visited the country thirty times. The king also expected much of Norway as a military resource. But Christian IV died a broken man. His foreign policy had failed and the Crown Prince died a year before his father. The Council of the Realm elected his younger son, Frederik, to be king and he had to accept a strict coronation charter which guaranteed the power of the Council of the Realm and the privileges of the nobility. Twelve years later, however, Frederik III was to win a resounding political victory over the Council of the Realm and the nobility. We shall now look more closely at Christian's defeat and Frederik's victory.

The Struggle for Power in Scandinavia in the First Half of the 17th Century

Early in the 17th century Denmark-Norway had the upper hand over its arch-rival, Sweden. This can be seen from a glance at the map. Gothenburg was the Swedes' only outlet to the North Sea and the Danish king controlled Øresund, where he collected customs duties. The so-called «naval stores» of the Baltic states – linen, hemp, tar, pitch and timber – were shipped through this bottleneck. The naval powers, England and Holland, depended on these stores and Øresund came into political focus. The northern borders had never been defined. Norwegians, Swedes

and Russians all imposed taxes on the Sami people and it became Sweden's goal to gain control of the north and fight her way out of the Danish-Norwegian encirclement.

When Christian IV had Magnus Lagabøte's law translated from Old Norse in 1604, he made changes in the defence arrangements. The old conscription law was not efficient enough. The king still had the right to conscript the common people when there was danger of war, but the farmers were now obliged to provide their own weapons. Each farm over a certain size was to have a rifle, a sword, an axe, bullets and gunpowder. The farmers had to congregate each year so that the king's men could inspect the weapons and the men.

In the Kalmar War (1611–13), Christian tried to stop the Swedish advance in the Baltic and in the north, and demanded that Norway should raise a conscript army of 8000 men. The Norwegian effort was hopeless. The Danish lords had little experience as military officers and the farmer soldiers lacked food and sufficient weapons. Many drank, fought and shot wildly and the officers were unable to prevent mass desertions.

This desertion has been forgotten in Norwegian tradition, but the battle of Kringen in Gudbrandsdalen is still remembered. Here a Norwegian farmer army defeated 300–400 Scottish mercenaries leaving only 113 survivors. Most of the prisoners of war were massacred the next day. This defeat of the Scots lived on in folk tradition in the centuries that followed and has meant much for Norwegian national pride.

The Kalmar War ended well for Christian IV. The peace treaty laid down that the coastline between Tysfjord and Varanger was Norwegian territory. This was thanks to the efforts of the Danish-Norwegian fleet and Danish action on Swedish territory. However, the war demonstrated one thing about Norway as a military resource. It was *possible* to raise a large farmer army.

Against the will of the Council of the Realm, Christian IV joined the Thirty Years' War (1618–48) on the side of the Protestants. In 1625 he declared war in his capacity as German duke but suffered a disastrous defeat and only just managed to keep the kingdom in one piece at the peace treaty four years later. The Swedes fared better and won great victories on German soil.

The war affected the Norwegian population, too. Over 3000 Norwegians were conscripted to serve in the Danish-Norwegian fleet and the border forts had permanent garrisons of 350 men. In 1628 the king issued a War Order for Norway. This Order was the foundation of the Norwegian army. The country was divided into districts of four large farms and each district was obliged to provide and equip one soldier. The system would have provided over 6000 infantry soldiers, but because the peace treaty was signed in 1629 the order was not implemented. It nevertheless provided the basis for a national defence force later on and Christian IV managed to utilise Norway as a resource in this war. Taxation was increased and customs duties from Norway made a welcome contribution to the treasury.

Christian did not remain passive in the following years, however. He needed to increase his revenues, so he increased the Øresund customs duties. This led to a coalition between Sweden and the Netherlands in 1640. Her wartime successes had given Sweden a place among the great powers of Europe. In this situation, a Danish nobleman, Hannibal Sehested, came to Norway as governor in 1642. He was the king's son-in-law and confidant and in spite of his 34 years was an experienced diplomat and linguist. He was to lead the organisation of the army. The order of 1628 was to be implemented and officers and weaponry brought from abroad. All this led to even heavier taxes on the farmers. The authorities had never made such demands on them before.

Just before Christmas 1643, well-trained Swedish troops marched north through

CHRISTIAN IV 1588-1988

NORGE 10.00

Jutland, which was soon occupied. Christian IV gathered his troops for battle in the rest of the country. Hannibal Sehested's Norwegian army did not win any great victories but Norwegian troops made a series of border attacks in southern Norway, which tied up the Swedish troops. Although the organisation was better this time, the soldiers were still unreliable and many went home. Farmers on both sides of the border agreed to leave each other alone! Most people felt that this was not their war but the Governor's war. It has since been called «Hannibal's quarrel». «The Norwegians are hard to rely on in a difficult situation», the Governor complained. At the peace in 1645 the king had to give up the islands of Gotland and Øsel and the Norwegian districts of Jemtland and Herjedalen, and the Netherlands obtained reductions in the Øresund customs duties.

The War of Revenge led by King Frederik III in 1657–60 was also a catastrophe. Norway lost Båhuslen and Denmark had to give up the districts east of Øresund. This happened in spite of fair Norwegian efforts and Jemtland was retaken for a while. For the first time, Norway had made a considerable contribution to the defence of the dual monarchy, but in 1660 Sweden's place as the great power of Scandinavia was still undisputed.

After the peace of 1660 Denmark-Norway faced an acute financial crisis. The kings had borrowed money for the war from rich citizens in Copenhagen and it was up to Frederik III to solve the problem.

The Scottish army lands at Romsdalen during the Kalmar War. Painting by A. Tidemand and M. Müller, 1876.

4 A busy King

Between 1536 and 1814 Denmark-Norway had ten kings called either Christian or Frederik. Only one of them, King Christian IV, is generally remembered today. He reigned for 60 years and stories of his marriages, his women and numerous legitimate and illegitimate children are well known. The King was fond of feasting and drinking, but he also wanted to govern his realm well. He was well-educated and trained to lead from an early age. As King, he was highly interested in everything that went on, both at court and throughout Denmark-Norway.

In Norway the King was primarily known for his interest in developing the country. Christian regarded Norway as a rich country. He brought in iron and mining experts from Germany. There was iron ore in the Norwegian mountains, and possibly copper, silver and gold too! The state could also earn revenues from forestry and fishing. They would be welcome in the struggle against the main enemy, Sweden, since King Christian intended to strengthen the position of Denmark-Norway as a great power in the North.

Christian IV was a warrior king, but he had bad luck in war. At the Peace of Brømsebro in 1645 he had to cede the Norwegian district of Jemtland and Herjedalen to Sweden. When the King died three years later the country was deeply in debt and Sweden was on the way to becoming the main power in Scandinavia.

Christian IV (1577–1648) became king when he was 11 years old and governed Denmark-Norway from the time he came of age in 1596. This portrait was painted by Peter Isaacz just after the Kalmar War (1611–13), when Christian had experienced some success. The King is wearing the sash of a field marshal.

The King often took part in meetings of the Supreme Court in Denmark and Norway. He was the supreme judge and took his work seriously. He had the common law of Magnus Lagabøte translated from Old Norse to Danish in 1604.
In this drawing by Karel v. Mander of 1648 King Christian is seated at the end of the table.

Christian IV visited Norway about 30 times. The map shows some of the places he visited most often. He was particularly interested in mining.

Vardø (1)

Kildin

JEMTLAND

HERJE-
DALEN

IDRE OG
SÄRNA

Bergen (5)

Akershus (11)

Kongsberg (3)

Flekkerøy (6)   Båhus (6)

In 1599 the King sailed along the Norwegian coast as far as the island of Kildin, now in the Soviet Union. He wanted to ensure control of Northern Norway.

700 ⟋ I 1000 riksdaler

600

500

400

300

200

100

0

- Customs duties
- New taxes
- Income from the fiefdoms

1600-1620 1621-24 1625-29 1630-40 1641-48 1649-1656

State revenues from Norway 1600–1656

Norwegian farmers were heavily taxed during the reign of King Christian IV. The King imposed new taxes and they were particularly high when Denmark-Norway was at war, i.e. in 1625–1629 (the Imperial War) and in 1643–1645 (the Torstensson War). Customs duties accounted for an increasingly large proportion of state revenues in Norway and Christian IV employed more customs officers so that collection would be more efficient. Income from the fiefdoms included land rent, ground rent, land taxes, fines and tithes. The statistics are from Øystein Rian, 1984.

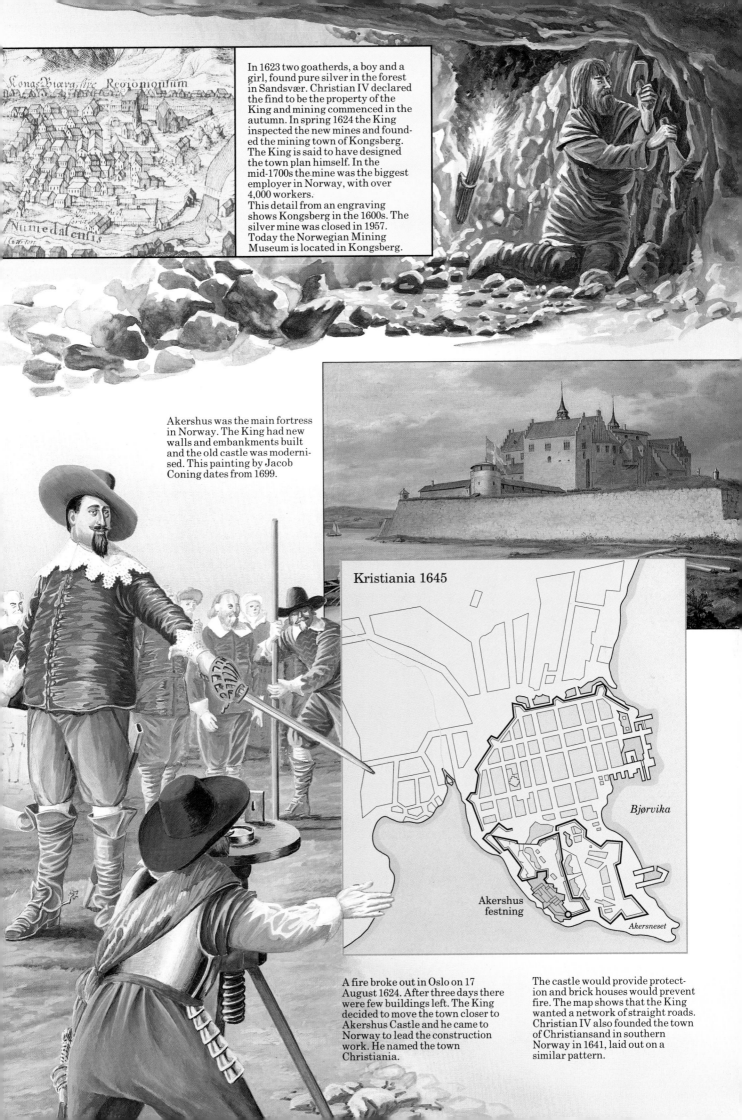

In 1623 two goatherds, a boy and a girl, found pure silver in the forest in Sandsvær. Christian IV declared the find to be the property of the King and mining commenced in the autumn. In spring 1624 the King inspected the new mines and founded the mining town of Kongsberg. The King is said to have designed the town plan himself. In the mid-1700s the mine was the biggest employer in Norway, with over 4,000 workers.

This detail from an engraving shows Kongsberg in the 1600s. The silver mine was closed in 1957. Today the Norwegian Mining Museum is located in Kongsberg.

Akershus was the main fortress in Norway. The King had new walls and embankments built and the old castle was modernised. This painting by Jacob Coning dates from 1699.

Kristiania 1645

Bjørvika

Akershus festning

Akersneset

A fire broke out in Oslo on 17 August 1624. After three days there were few buildings left. The King decided to move the town closer to Akershus Castle and he came to Norway to lead the construction work. He named the town Christiania.

The castle would provide protection and brick houses would prevent fire. The map shows that the King wanted a network of straight roads. Christian IV also founded the town of Christiansand in southern Norway in 1641, laid out on a similar pattern.

Norway and the Absolute Monarchy

The Council of the Realm and the nobility had been losing their authority for several generations. We have previously seen how the overlords gradually lost their powers and the wars had shown that the nobility no longer played a military role. However, it was the financial crisis of 1660 that broke them for good. At an autumn meeting of the three estates in Copenhagen, the king supported the representatives of the Danish bourgeoisie, who were thirsting for political power. He imprisoned the Council of the Realm and the nobility in hostile Copenhagen until they gave way. The result of this was that Frederik III and his successors obtained hereditary rights to the throne of Denmark and the king was empowered to design a constitution for Denmark-Norway. The Council of the Realm ceased to exist and all power lay in the hands of the king. He had become an absolute monarch.

Norway was on the periphery of events in the autumn of 1660 and the Norwegians were not represented at the homage ceremony in Copenhagen in October. However, the following year there was a separate homage ceremony in Christiania, where Frederik was represented by his son, Prince Christian. Of the 543 representatives, 408 were farmers. This shows the special position of Norwegian farmers in relation to their opposite numbers in Denmark. Only a handful of farmers took part in Copenhagen and only one of them was allowed to kiss the king's hand.

After 1660 both the central and the local administration were reorganised. Whereas prior to 1660 the union had had only one administrative office for state affairs, now a system similar to present-day ministries was introduced, affairs being distributed according to subject matter. These *collegiates* also included representatives of the bourgeoisie. The nobility had lost their monopoly of power. The fiefdoms were replaced by shires, headed by a district governor on a permanent salary. The shires were sub-divided into bailiwicks. The king did not wish the district governors to become too powerful. Military officials were therefore put in charge of the army. All officials were appointed by the king and there were approximately 1600 of them in Norway at the time of the absolute monarchy. They included district governors, judges, bailiffs, clergymen, military, officers and customs officials. The collegiates led the local administration from Copenhagen, with the king and his advisers at the top. However, it was a long way to the capital and the opinions of the Norwegian officials were influential in the handling of matters affecting Norway.

Rural Society

In the period between 1500 and 1800 the population of Norway increased from about 150,000 to 900,000 and nine out of ten people were associated with rural society. The disappearance of the plagues was the main reason for the growth in population, but mortality was still high particularly among children. As late as the 18th century, nearly one quarter of all newborn infants died in the first year of their lives.

From the end of the 17th century, Norwegian farmers were given title to the lands they farmed. When the absolute monarchy was introduced in 1660, only 20 per cent of the land was owned by the farmers but by 1800 nearly 60 per cent of the land was in the hands of those who farmed it.

In order to repay the state debt, King Frederick III had given land to the merchants to whom he owed money. They soon resold it, to the farmers, who mortgaged their farms to buy it. In this way the townsfolk liberated capital which they could invest in other ventures, while the farmers were able to buy their own land. Property rights gave security and the right to free timber in the forests that belonged to the individual farms. Only in northern Norway did the landowners retain title to land because of the hunting and fishing rights that went with the farms.

The increase in population after 1500 led

to cheat the fishermen. Stones on the scales and falsified records were commonplace. Debts were passed down from father to son and the authorities were unable to resolve the situation. The merchants retained their power and position throughout the Union Period.

The growth of Norwegian shipping must be seen in the light of the increase in trade. Although Norway exported considerable quantities of goods throughout the Middle Ages, most had been shipped on foreign vessels, mainly Hanseatic, Dutch, British and Danish. In the 1600s the authorities tried to encourage Norwegian shipping by means of economic incentives. One example is the defence ships, which paid reduced customs tariffs. But it was not until the wars in Europe towards the end of the 17th century that Norwegian ships got their real chance and the years from 1690 to 1710 have been called the «first golden age» of Norwegian shipping. Denmark-Norway had remained neutral at that time. After Frederik IV became involved in the Great Scandinavian War in 1709, however, business went badly and the foreigners were once more in control after the peace treaty of 1720.

It was not until the Revolutionary Wars in the second half of the 18th century that Norwegian shipowners had a second chance. Neutrality was once again profitable and when the Union was drawn into the Napoleonic wars in 1807, Norway had become one of the most important shipping nations in Europe. The Norwegian fleet was as large as those of Denmark and the Duchies of Schleswig and Holstein combined and once again the town merchants skimmed the cream.

The growth of the towns and commercial prosperity were, of course, closely intertwined. At that time a town was called a *kjøpstad* (trading place) and in 1660 only eight towns had this status. In 1800 there were 23 towns in Norway.

A town was a complicated society. At the top were the patrician merchants and the officials. The most prominent citizens lived in great luxury. They constructed

beautiful buildings, such as *Stiftsgården* in Trondheim. An English visitor in 1799 wrote that although it was built of wood, it was the most impressive palace in the whole of Scandinavia. And social life flourished. After a visit to John Collett at Ullevål Gård in Christiania the same Englishman wrote: «*Such was the magnificence of the feast to which we had been invited, that it would hardly be possible for our own Sovereign to afford a more sumptuous entertainment.*» The officials were far less well-off than the patricians but their office brought status and authority and many married into the upper classes.

Tradesmen and craftsmen were also part of the bourgeoisie, although they came well below the patricians and the group included very different social strata. There was a difference between a master baker with many apprentices and small shopkeepers or cobblers who plied their trade in the back streets. Over half of the inhabitants in any town did not belong to the bourgeosie at all. They were servant girls, day labourers, soldiers, prostitutes and the poor.

The biggest wooden building in Scandinavia, Stiftsgården, Trondheim, was built for Cecilia Christine de Schöller in the 1770s. Today it is one of the royal family's residences.

The runebom was a drum used by the Sami people to contact the animistic gods.

A missionary preaching to the Sami people in the 1700s.

These drawings of 1555 by the Swedish historian Olaus Magnus show that the Sami people were good at hunting and skiing.

The Sami people

The Roman historian, Tacitus, was the first to write about the Sami people. In *Germania,* he wrote that the Sami people were good hunters. From the Viking Age onwards the Sami people had to pay taxes to Norwegian chieftains and kings.

From the Middle Ages the Sami people lived in *siidas.* A *siida* was an area around a fjord or a river. People in the *siida* cooperated in hunting, trapping and fishing. From the 16th century some of the Sami began to keep flocks of tame reindeer, while others ceased their nomadic existence and gained their livelihood from farming and fishing. In the 18th and 19th centuries the Sami lands were divided among Denmark-Norway, Sweden and Russia. In Norway the conversion of the Sami people to Christianity began at the beginning of the 18th century and the old animistic religion disappeared. At the end of the 19th century the Storting decided that Sami children should be taught in Norwegian. An Act passed in 1902 made it difficult for Sami people to buy land. Only after the Second World War were these policies changed.

Elsa Laula Renberg (1877–1931) tried to organise the Sami people at the beginning of the 20th century.

In 1989 King Olav V opened the first popularly elected Sami assembly. It is called the *Sameting* and meets in Karasjok. The aim of the *Sameting* is to protect the Sami language and culture, and the assembly cooperates with other indigenous populations all over the world.

Njåem
Dot
Gærhkoe
Troàn'din
(Trondheim) ● Ladtie
(Kristiansund) ● Tjohkele
(Ålesund)
(Røros)

Sami language areas

The Sami people speak nine different dialects. Many of them differ so greatly that the Sami cannot understand each other. The map shows the various language areas, which cross national borders.

In 1990 there were between 30,000 and 40,000 Sami living in Norway. There were approximately 17,000 in Sweden, 6000 in Finland and 2000 in the Soviet Union.

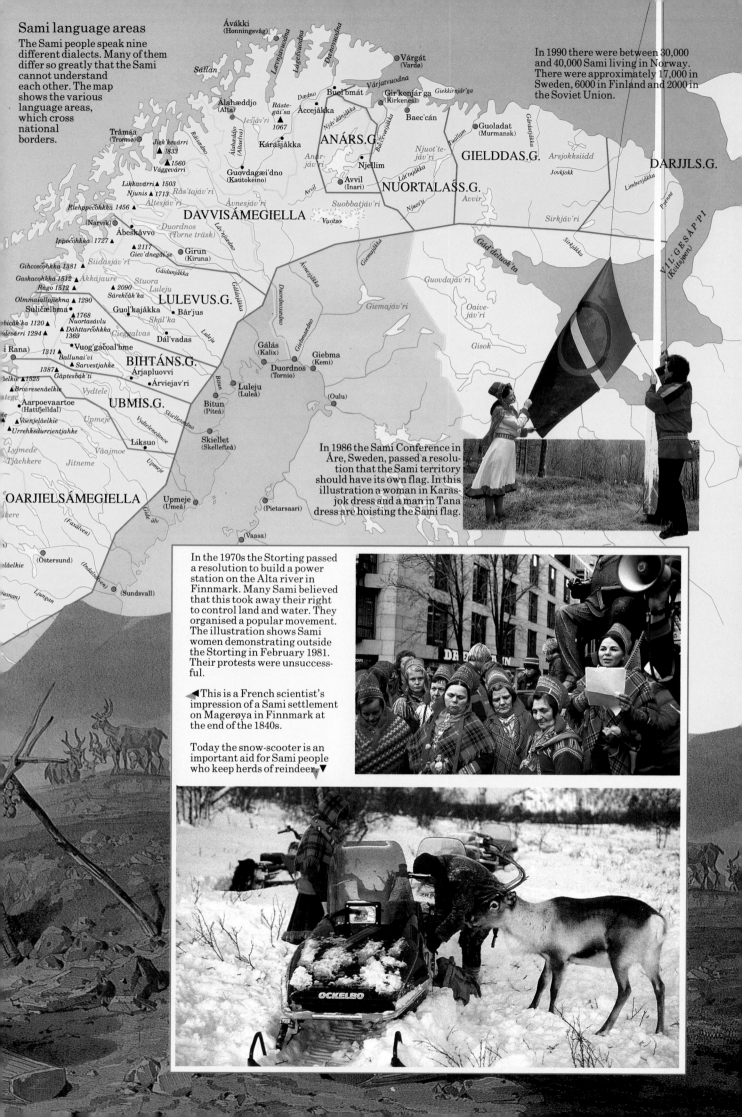

Map labels:

Ávákki (Honningsvåg)
Várgát (Vardø)
Sállan
Lævnjatvuodna
Lágešvuodna
Dænovuodna
Várjatvuodna
Dødno
Buol'bmát
Gir'konjár'ga (Kirkenes)
Giekkirnjár'ga
Álahæddjo (Alta)
Ráste-gái'sa
Accejåkka
Niáv'dánjåkka
Bæc'cán
Bác'čevejåkka
Guoladat (Murmansk)
Gåradajåkka
Tråmsa (Tromsø)
Jesjáv'ri
1067
ANÁRS.G.
Njuot'te-jáv'ri
Uallom
GIELDDAS.G.
Arsjokksiidd
Jiek'kevárri 1833
Álahædjo (Alaheatvu)
Kárásjåkka
Anár-jáv'ri
Njellim
Læt'tujåkka
Jovkjokk
Avvir
DARJJLS.G.
1560 Vággevárri
Guovdagæi'dno (Kautokeino)
Njuortasåvlu
Avvil (Inari)
NUORTALASS.G.
Likkavárri 1503
Råås'tojáv'ri
Avvil
Njuot'ti
Sirkjáv'ri
Limbesjåkka
Pkene
Njunis 1713
Áltesjáv'ri
Ávnesjáv'ri
Suobbatjáv'ri
Vuotso
Riehppeeohkka 1456
DAVVISÁMEGIELLA
Duordnos (Torne träsk)
Lás'njiaedno
Giemajåkka
Gåd'deluok'ta
Sirkjåkka
VIL'GE SÁP'PI (Kvikjspen)
(Narvik)
Ábeskávvo
Ávnesjåkka
Duordnoseduno
Giemajáv'ri
Guovdajáv'ri
Oaive-jáv'ri
Ippoeohkka 1727
2117 Giev'dnegái'se
Girun (Kiruna)
Gisok
Gihccecohkka 1381
Siidasjáv'ri
Gáidunjåkka
G.
Gaskacohkka 1512 Åkkájaure
Giebmaardno
Stuora Luleju
Rago 1512
2090 Sárekčák'ka
LULEVUS.G.
Olmmaiallojiekna 1290
Skål'ka
Gálás (Kalix)
Suličælbma
1768 Nuortasávlu
Guol'kajåkka
Bår'jus
Giebma (Kemi)
devárri 1294 Dáhttarčohkka 1369
Ciegqalvas
Dál'vadas
Luleju
bicåk'ka 1120
Vuog'gačoal'bme
Duordnos (Tornio)
i Rana) 1311
Ballunai'vi
BIHTÁNS.G.
Luleju (Luleå)
Sarvestjahke
Árjapluovvi
Bitun
(Oulu)
1387 Gáptesbák'ti
Árviejav'ri
Bitun (Piteå)
elkie 1525
Browresenælkie
UBMIS.G.
ategé
Aarpoevaartoe (Hattfjelldal)
Vydtele
Liksuo
Skiellet (Skellefteå)
Vøenjelåelkie
Vydtelenatinoe
Urrehksdurrientjahke
Upmeje
Lyjmede
Våajmoe
Upmeje
Tjáehkere
Jitneme
OARJIELSÁMEGIELLA
Upmeje
Upmeje (Umeå)
(Faxälven)
(Pietarsaari)
elkie
(Östersund)
(Indälsälven)
Vaasa
usnan)
(Sundsvall)
Ljungan

In 1986 the Sami Conference in Åre, Sweden, passed a resolution that the Sami territory should have its own flag. In this illustration a woman in Karasjok dress and a man in Tana dress are hoisting the Sami flag.

In the 1970s the Storting passed a resolution to build a power station on the Alta river in Finnmark. Many Sami believed that this took away their right to control land and water. They organised a popular movement. The illustration shows Sami women demonstrating outside the Storting in February 1981. Their protests were unsuccessful.

◀ This is a French scientist's impression of a Sami settlement on Magerøya in Finnmark at the end of the 1840s.

Today the snow-scooter is an important aid for Sami people who keep herds of reindeer ▼

Warrior-king Karl XII being carried home to Sweden by faithful soldiers in December 1718. Painting by G. Cederstrøm, 1878.

Stability and Growth in the 18th Century.

In the first twenty years of the 18th century there was unrest in the Scandinavian countries. The Great Scandinavian War broke out in 1700 but Denmark-Norway did not become seriously involved until 1709. After a number of victories, Sweden's young, warlike King Karl XII had suffered a serious defeat at Poltava in the Ukraine and King Frederik IV now entered the battle to win back old Danish-Norwegian territory. The King attacked Skåne but the campaign was unsuccessful and Karl was once again on the offensive. In 1716 and 1718 the Swedes advanced on southern Norway. King Karl XII fell at the siege of Halden in December 1718. A Norwegian or Swedish bullet had stopped his warlike career.

The war cost both countries dearly. The citizens of Halden had set fire to 330 houses to stop the enemy. Sweden had to give up its exemption from customs duties at Øresund, and all the Swedish possessions in the Baltic states and Germany were lost. Denmark-Norway did not regain any territory but Sweden's period as a great power was over and the balance was restored.

The goal of the absolute monarchy was to join the two countries in economic, political and cultural union with Copenhagen at the centre. The results of this policy were clearly seen in the 18th century. Approximately one third of Norwegian state revenues were transferred to Denmark. All areas of the Norwegian administration were directly subordinate to the central authorities in Denmark. However, the authorities listened to the advice given by the officials in Norway and most people did not feel oppressed. There was legal security and all citizens had the right to present their case to the King by means of a petition. The district magistrates were even obliged to help ordinary people write their petitions and thousands were sent to Copenhagen every year. The petitions contained everything from requests for pardon and exemption from taxation to complaints about officials. The farmers trusted that the King, «the father himself» would cut through the red tape and uphold the rights of the people. The Copenhagen authorities read and listened and usually followed a policy which satisfied the wishes of the people.

But of course there were conflicts. We have already heard of the unrest at the Kongsberg and Røros mines. For the last twenty years of the 18th century the farmer Christian Jensen Lofthus and the evangelist Hans Nielsen Hauge carried on a battle with the authorities in their own separate fields. Lofthus complained to the king about the way in which officials and townspeople in Agder exploited the farmers and he became the leader of a widespread farmers' rebellion. He sat chained to a stone pillar in Akershus Castle for eleven years and died there in 1797. His life sentence was upheld by the Supreme Court only two years after his death. The authorities nevertheless reacted to the demands made by Lofthus. Officials were relieved from their posts and the regulations were changed. Hans Nielsen Hauge fought for the right to be able to preach the word of God freely, where the ministers of the state church had a monopoly. The number of his supporters grew rapidly to become a natio-

nal uprising. Hauge was also kept in prison for years without a legal sentence but
no-one managed to break the movement he
had founded. Common to Lofthus and
Hauge was that both fought against the
local authorities in Norway, not the King
or the Union. The Union with Denmark
was accepted by most people.

The citizenry and the officials had other
complaints. They criticized centralisation
and compared Copenhagen to a bloodsuck-
ing leech. There were several demands for
a separate Norwegian bank and a Norwegian university but the king refused.
This refusal was most probably due to the
fear that acceding to these requests might
lead to the dissolution of the Union. The
upper classes were aware of events in the
rest of Europe and it is not surprising that
nationalism flourished in these circles. A
sense of national identity was also nurtur-
ed by the Norwegian Society in Copenhagen, which was a meeting place for
Norwegian authors and students.

In spite of self-assertion and growing
nationalism, however, there was little
danger of Denmark and Norway parting
company in the 18th century. In the 1790s
the government followed a liberalist policy and various measures served to temper
the criticism of the citizenry. The good
times at the turn of the century further
quenched the citizens' discontent. The
Union did not show signs of dissolution
until both countries were drawn into the
Napoleonic Wars.

*«The Haugians», paint-
ing by A. Tidemand,
1852.*

*Eilif Peterssen: «An
Evening at the Norwe-
gian Society, 1780»,
painted in 1892.*

1814 - INDEPEN-DENCE AND A NEW UNION

The British frigate «Tartar» in battle with Norwegian gunboats outside the gunpowder factory at Alvøen, Bergen, in 1808.

«It was called a year (....), but centuries have run their course and been far less remarkable than this one year. I do not think the history of any other country ever saw its like. Even the catastrophic fall of Napoleon is less astounding.»

Claus Pavels, chaplain at Akershus Castle, wrote these words in his diary for 1814, and with good reason. At the beginning of the year, the union of Denmark and Norway was intact, and the joint kingdoms were ruled by one absolute monarch. For a few hectic summer months Norway was an independent realm with a king of her own and a constitution founded on the sovereignty of the people. In the autumn, the country was forced into a new union, this time with Sweden.

Denmark-Norway chooses Napoleon

In 1792 France declared war on Austria and Prussia, and Europe was still at war in 1814. Denmark-Norway managed to remain neutral. The economic ups and downs caused by the war were exploited in both of the kingdoms, and the bourgeoisie in Norway made fortunes. At the time there was talk of «a golden age» in shipping and the export trades.

However, it was difficult to stay clear of the maelstrom. State after state found itself obliged to choose one of the main protagonists – the Emperor Napoleon Bonaparte of France or the sea power Great Britain. As the British were anxious to prevent neutral ships carrying goods to France, British warships searched Dano-Norwegian merchant vessels. In order to protect this trade, the Danish King had the ships move in convoy, accompanied by a warship. This provocative practice was swiftly brought to an end by the British: a British naval force attacked Copenhagen in 1801. After a brief and bloody battle the British were able to inspect the cargoes of Dano-Norwegian merchant ships unimpeded.

In September 1807 the British struck again. Troops went ashore on Sjaelland, and warships bombarded Copenhagen. The British confiscated most of the Dano-Norwegian fleet, 37 large ships and some smaller ones, to make sure they did not fall into Napoleon's hands. This episode marked the end of a century of peace for Denmark-Norway. Eleven days later, King Frederik VI decided to ally himself with Napoleon, a decision which proved disastrous for Norway because Denmark and Norway were now committed to participating in the blockade of Great Britain. King Frederik succeeded in averting an attack by Napoleon on Denmark and the duchies of Schleswig and Holstein, but for Norway the agreement meant first and foremost a halt to supplies from abroad.

Opposite page: O. Wergeland: «The Constituent Assembly at Eidsvoll», painting 1855. The leader of the Independence Party, Christian Magnus Falsen, is standing by the table. Seated on his right, the secretary of the Constituent Assembly, Wilhelm K. F. Christie. Between them on the other side of the table, Count Herman Wedel-Jarlsberg. The painting now hangs in the Storting in Oslo.

Jean Baptiste Berna-dotte at the Battle of Halle, 1806. In 1810 he became Crown Prince of Norway, taking the name Karl Johan. Painting by Justien Clary, 1841.

War and Blockade

Norway, then, faced problems in the war with Great Britain, as Norwegian ships were prevented from exporting timber, fish and iron, and the transport of corn from Denmark, crucial to Norway, was reduced drastically. The situation forced the King to abandon his unitary policies for the two kingdoms. Government of Norway was, for the duration of the blockade, vested in a governing commission set up in Christiania. Norway became completely isolated in 1808, when war broke out between Denmark-Norway and Sweden. Earlier that year Russia had won Finland from Sweden, and the Swedish King Gustav IV Adolf saw acquisition of Norway as compensation for that loss. But he was thwarted. The Norwegian soldier-farmers defended themselves successfully and defeated the Swedes in several minor battles in southern Norway. At the end of the year a ceasefire was agreed, and when peace was signed in 1809, all was as before between Denmark-Norway and Sweden.

The loss of Finland and the failure of the campaign against Norway created widespread dissatisfaction with the King in Sweden, and Gustav IV Adolf had to relinquish the throne. His old, childless and senile uncle was elected king in his stead, as Karl XIII. It was clear that Sweden needed a forceful heir to the throne. The choice fell on one of Napoleon's generals, Jean Baptiste Bernadotte, who, on his arrival in Sweden as Crown Prince in 1810, took the name Karl Johan. Thereafter, the Crown Prince was the Swedes' undisputed leader, and his objective was conquest of Norway.

Both the middle and lower classes suffered hard times in the years following 1807. That year Norwegian shipowners lost 553 ships, either confiscated in British ports or seized by British warships. The export of timber diminished dramatically: in 1808 the volume shipped from Norwegian harbours was only one per cent of what it had been in 1805. For the export of fish there was a corresponding decline. South-eastern Norway was hardest hit, because it was dependent on corn from Denmark. 40 % of the country's population lived in the county of Akershus, and the death rate there rose markedly, from an average of 8278 people per year for 1803–7 to 12,679 in 1808 and 21,391 in 1809.

The governing commission in Norway had on several occasions demanded that the King alter his foreign policy, but Frederik VI stood by his decision in favour of the alliance with Napoleon and the British blockade. However, in the summer of 1809 the King realised that the famine and discontent in Norway could split the union, and so he permitted Norway to resume selling timber to Britain in return for the British allowing the corn ships to pass freely between Norway and Denmark. This «trade by licence» saved the merchant class in Norway from ruin, and the population of the south-east from death by famine. The crisis was over, for the time being.

In 1812 Napoleon attacked his former ally, Russia. The widening of the war compelled Frederik VI to rescind his licences to trade. That summer was exceptionally cold in the south-east of the country, and harvests were minimal. In the north, the fishing season proved disastrous, and crops perished in the cold. There was famine and need throughout the country; many died. In several areas the peasant farmers revolted, but as on the earlier occasions when they had been led by Christian Jensen Lofthus and by Hans Nielsen Hauge, their dissatisfaction was directed at merchants and public officials, not at the King and his foreign policy.

Napoleon's defeat in Russia was the beginning of the end for Napoleon himself and also for the twin realm of Denmark-Norway. Sweden joined the ranks of Napoleon's enemies, and the Great Powers promised Karl Johan Norway, provided he helped crush France. Following the victory at the battle of Leipzig in 1813, Karl Johan turned aside and marched on Denmark. After brief hostilities, Frederik VI had to admit defeat, and on 14 January 1814 he signed a peace treaty at Kiel. In it he ceded Norway to the King of Sweden.

Prince Christian Frederik and the Constitution

When the news of the Treaty of Kiel reached Norway, the country had the very person to lead it: Prince Christian Frederik, heir to the throne of Denmark-Norway and appointed Governor of Norway by the king in 1813. The prince was only 26 years old, and lacked military or administrative experience, but he was gifted, hardworking, handsome and charming. His prime duty was to secure the union with Denmark, for the King and for himself.

Christian Frederik refused to accept the Treaty of Kiel, and immediately set about strengthening his position in Norway. In public, the King was bound by the agreement he had signed at Kiel, but in confidence he supported his heir's plans, thinking that the Norwegian throne was perhaps not lost, after all. A few days after concluding the Treaty of Kiel, the King secretly gave permission for the corn ships to sail to Norway. His double-dealing had to be concealed from the Swedes and the British.

Christian Frederik's chief opponent in

Christian Frederik, painted by J. L. Lund, 1813.

Norway was Count Herman Wedel Jarlsberg. Throughout the years of the blockade and of hardship, Wedel had worked to achieve a union of Norway and Sweden, believing that only lasting peace with Sweden and Great Britain would assure the country's export trade and corn supplies. Though convinced that union with Sweden would benefit merchant and farmer alike, he and his adherents wished for a considerable degree of independence for Norway. However, Christian Frederik's ideas won the day. The bonds with Denmark were still strong, and the prince had in his power the loyal office-holding elite in Norway. Karl Johan's agents were doing their best to sway people, but Christian Frederik's propaganda was more effective. He spoke and wrote of his «beloved Norwegian people», and of the country's «fortune and glory».

On 16 February Christian Frederik summoned twenty-one influential Norwegians to a meeting of «notables» at Eidsvoll. They were to consider the prince's claim that he was entitled to the throne, and his wish to be an absolute monarch. But their view was quite different: they were in favour of a liberal constitution, and a king elected by the people. It was clear to everyone that Christian Frederik was the obvious candidate, but he had to accept that his royal power was in the gift of the people.

Christian Frederik agreed to the meeting's demands, and it was resolved that the people should now elect delegates to a constituent assembly to be held at Eidsvoll. Voters and the representatives elected would, it was decided, be obliged to swear a «people's oath» to the effect that they would work for Norway's independence. Meanwhile, Christian Frederik was to rule the country as Regent.

Early in April the first delegates arrived at Eidsvoll. On Easter Day, Christian Frederik and the representatives of the people met for a church service, and on the following day, 11 April, Christian Frederik opened the national assembly. Of its 112 members, 18 were merchants, 37 peasant freeholders, and 57 public officials in civil, ecclesiastical or military posts. The prince did not take part in the assembly's deliberations, but he stayed at Eidsvoll and influenced its decisions. He was, after all, in a position to make demands: if the constitution did not please him, he could refuse the crown.

The delegates at the national assembly divided into two factions. The larger was the Independence Party, loyal supporters of Christian Frederik's policies and led by Christian Magnus Falsen, a magistrate. The other faction was the Unionist Party, mainly rich merchants and headed by Count Wedel Jarlsberg. The Unionists were of the opinion that the Treaty of Kiel could not be brushed aside and that a Swedish solution was unavoidable.

The delegates at Eidsvoll took six weeks to draw up a constitution for Norway. They used as models several foreign constitutions which had come into being during the Revolutionary and Napoleonic periods, but in the event they were most influenced by the French Constitution.

The sovereignty of the people was the guiding principle of the constitution they created. Power was shared among the national assembly (to be called the Storting), the judiciary, and the king in accordance with Montesquieu's principles, but it was characteristic that the king's share was substantial. He was the supreme military commander, and could declare war and conclude peace. Furthermore he could levy taxes and appoint officials, and he had a delaying power of veto on proposed legislation. Originating legislation and granting funds were the duties of the Storting, but it was to assemble for only three months every third year unless the king decided otherwise. For its legislative work it was to divide into two chambers, the Odelsting and the Lagting. The franchise rules laid down in the constitution were very liberal by contemporary standards. Nearly half the male population over the age of 25 was given the vote, with the result that the landowning peasantry acquired political influence. No other country was able to match this. And so the constitution hammered out at Eidsvoll was a compromise between democracy and absolute monarchy.

On 17 May 1814 work on the Constitution had been completed, and the national assembly unanimously elected Christian Frederik King of a free, sovereign and independent Norway. Two days later the newly elected King attended the assembly and swore an oath on the Constitution. And on the following day the constituent assembly held its final meeting. The delegates linked hands and proclaimed their everlasting unity and loyalty.

Into Union with Sweden

Over the whole country an enthusiastic people celebrated the Constitution and the newly elected King. But danger was not far distant. The Great Powers suspected that Christian Frederik was double-dealing, and a new blockade put an end to the trade between Denmark and Norway. In continental Europe Napoleon had been defeated and Crown Prince Karl Johan was now free to put into effect the provisions of the Treaty of Kiel.

Christian Frederik tried to get the Great Powers to recognise an independent Norway but failed. At the end of July Karl Johan attacked the south of Norway with 40–50,000 experienced soldiers. Christian Frederik faced him with an army of 30,000 poorly trained soldiers, and the war was short. The Norwegians retreated, and at Moss on 14 August a ceasefire was agreed. Karl Johan accepted the Eidsvoll Constitution as the basis for negotiations and promised that the Swedes would not propose any amendments beyond those necessary to achieve the union of Norway with Sweden. He demanded that Christian Frederik should convene an extraordinary session of the Storting, renounce the throne and leave the country.

Karl Johan had his will. He avoided the need to ravage Norway, and all the bitterness that would have caused. Christian Frederik issued writs for an extraordinary

session of the Storting, and it met on 8 October in Christiania. Two days later the King abdicated and on the same afternoon he left Norway.

Without delay the Storting resolved that Norway should go into union with Sweden, and the negotiations began. On the whole their results were very satisfactory to the Norwegians. The new, revised Constitution stipulated that the Norwegian government must be split in two, with one part in Christiania and the other in Stockholm where the king resided. And Norway was to have no independent foreign policy. It was apparent that Norway was the inferior partner in the union, and yet the power of the king emerged diminished, compared with the Eidsvoll Constitution. He had lost the right to declare war and conclude peace without the approval of the Storting. Nor was he permitted to appoint Swedes to public office in Norway. Furthermore, Norway was to have her own flag and her own bank.

On 4 November the revised Constitution was ready, and the Storting elected Karl XIII as King of Norway.

Norwegian ski troops 1808, drawing by A. Bloch.

NORWAY
1814-1905

Crisis and the Struggle for Independence

After the end of the Napoleonic Wars, economic crisis hit Norway. The blockade had been lifted, but the timber trade with Britain took time to get under way again, and the British imposed a high duty on Norwegian timber, discriminating in favour of imports from Canada. These export difficulties for Norway affected shipping, and a great fire in the timber stores at Drammen in 1817 made the situation even worse. Most of the wealthy, established citizens went bankrupt as a result.

The exchequer felt the post-war crisis, too, because export duties were an important source of national revenue. And on top of all this, the young state of Norway suffered a severe bout of inflation. In the years prior to 1814 King Frederik VI had printed banknotes to finance the war, and Christian Frederik had done the same in 1814. Crown Prince Karl Johan followed all this closely from Sweden. Perhaps he hoped that the Norwegian government and the Storting, the national assembly, would not be able to find a way out of the financial crisis.

The Norwegians succeeded, albeit slowly. In 1816 the Storting introduced the spesidaler as a monetary unit and established the Bank of Norway, a central bank having the exclusive right to issue banknotes. The value of the spesidaler was to be assured by means of a capital stock of precious metals in the bank to the tune of 2 to 3 million spesidalers. The idea was that the nation should make voluntary contributions to the stock, but the will to give was rather weak, and the Storting imposed a «silver tax» to be paid by people with assets. Only silver was accepted, no banknotes. The middle and upper classes throughout the country had to part with their heirlooms, but progress was slow. The economic situation improved during the 1820s, yet not until 1842 had the Bank of Norway collected sufficient silver to be able to redeem the banknotes it had issued.

The Storting managed to preserve Norway's independence, even though the country was on the verge of national bankruptcy, and despite a further financial problem which exacerbated relations with Sweden. At the Treaty of Kiel, Karl Johan and King Frederik VI had agreed that Norway would pay her share of the joint national debt of Denmark-Norway, and by 1820 the Danes were pressing for their due. However, the Storting was unwilling to pay. Norway had never accepted the Treaty of Kiel, and the country was poor. The European Great Powers gave their support to Denmark, and Karl Johan, who had become King in 1818, warned the Storting: «If you wish to remain independent, pay your debt to Denmark». When in May 1821 the King announced that he was about to deploy 6000 soldiers in Christiania on military manoeuvres, the Storting feared a coup, and capitulated. A large majority voted that Norway should pay up.

In the autumn of that year, Karl Johan suggested several amendments to the Constitution. One was that the Storting should be convened only every five years, others that the king should have the right to dissolve the Storting and to appoint its presidents. Most disconcerting was the king's claim of an absolute veto on legislation. These proposals were made several times, and accompanied by threats of military action, but the Storting rejected them all. The delegates looked on the Constitution of 1814 as a safeguard against loss of liberty and extended royal power.

Another bone of contention was celebration of 17 May, the day on which the Constitution had been completed. Ever since 1814 there had been festivities, and the custom became more widespread during the 1820s. This displeased Karl Johan, who regarded 17 May as a day of rebellion, and considered 4 November, the date the union with Sweden was inaugurated, a more suitable day for celebrations. The Storting made an attempt to moderate the rejoicing to placate the King, but on 17 May 1829 there was a violent clash in Christiania. It was a warm Sunday, and a

Opposite page:
Håkon Kaulum
(1863–1933): «Bark in a
Storm», undated.

H. P. C. Dahm: «The Fire at the Timber Stores in Drammen on the Night of 1–2 May 1817».

crowd turned out to cheer the steamship «*Constitutionen*» as she dropped anchor. Peaceable though the crowd was, the town authorities sent soldiers to the main square to disperse it. Noone was killed, but the episode, which became known as the Battle of the Market Square, had lasting consequences. People vented their fury on the Swedish Governor, Balthazar von Platen, after this scandalous use of troops. Henceforth it was quite unthinkable that a Swede should be appointed Governor in Norway. And celebrating 17 May became normal practice. Once again the Norwegians had got the better of Karl Johan, and in the 1830s the conflict between them abated. When he died in 1844, King Karl Johan was actually popular in Norway.

Government by State Officials and a Storting of Freeholder Farmers

Norway after 1814 is often said to have belonged to her officials. Those who had held public office in the days of the absolute monarchy maintained their positions and their power: the county prefects, bailiffs, local magistrates, clergymen, military officers and university teachers. To them were now added the top civil servants in the new government departments, and the king's ministers. This class of officialdom numbered just under 2000, but had a dis-

proportionate degree of influence and authority. In country districts, the parish priest, the magistrate and the bailiff automatically assumed a leading role, and the local farmers elected them to the Storting. These officials were educated; most of them had studied in Copenhagen and had mastered Latin and the finer points of etiquette. They had professional knowhow. Members of this elite had drafted the Constitution, and it was no coincidence that according to the Constitution an official could not be dismissed. They were also better off than most people, and were qualified by their office to a place in the higher echelons of society. There was a cultural gulf between them and the farmers whose praises they had sung in the days of their intoxication with the idea of national independence, but whom they now considered to be «coarse».

It was the officials elected to the Storting who led the fight against Karl Johan's assault on the Constitution, for to defend the Constitution was to defend their authority in the state. Yet though they defeated the King, other dangers loomed. In the late 1820s, the farmers became a force to be reckoned with. Before the 1832 elections to the Storting, they were exhorted by their leaders to elect their own men to the Storting – and not the usual officials. This advice was heeded. Freeholder farmers were in the majority in the Storting which assembled the following year, and it has

since been called the Storting of Farmers. The next election also resulted in a majority of farmers.

These new members had two main points on their agenda. In the first place they were anxious to cut public spending and make taxes as low as possible. Many spoke disparagingly of the administrative class which produced nothing and lived off the labour of others. The Storting of Farmers reduced taxes and increased the import duty on many goods, so transferring much of the burden from rural districts to the towns. The farmers, who were by and large self-sufficient, felt that developing the country's infrastructure was not of direct benefit to them, and they resented the armed forces because conscription applied only to men from the agricultural classes.

The second point was local self-government. In 1833 a group of farmers proposed that each municipality should be governed by a small committee of elected representatives, a municipal executive board. The aim was to reduce the influence of public officials over the local community, and the proposal was adopted. In 1837 an Act relating to municipal executive boards was passed. An elected local council was empowered to decide certain matters,

concerning the schoolhouse, teachers' pay, local roads and care of the poor, for example. Central government could also impose tasks on it, and in fact did so to an increasing extent. At first participation in local elections was small, but it picked up in the second half of the century. Local self-government gave the farmers valuable political experience.

At the election of 1838 they lost their majority in the Storting. Once again officeholders were elected.

N. Hertzberg: «Farmhouse Interior. Wedding in Kinsarvik in the 1820s.»

H. E. Reimers: «The Battle of the Market Square», the main Square in Christiania, Sunday 17 May 1829.

A Golden Age in Literature

When in the autumn of 1814 Norway entered the union with Sweden, she was permitted to keep the Constitution. Norwegians saw it as a defence against Sweden. Great challenges faced the newly-fledged nation in most spheres of life. In the field of the arts, identifying what was quintessentially Norwegian became of prime importance. What should be the written language in the land? Had there during all the years of Danish rule been anything one could call Norwegian literature? Was there typically Norwegian music? What did Norway and its rural population look like? The artists set off from the towns on journeys of discovery, and brought back with them to the urban public their impressions of Norwegian landscape and folk life.

The drawing shows the manor at Eid voll where the Norwegian Constituti was adopted. 112 officials, merchant and farmers assembled here in the spring of 1814. Together they gave Norway one of Europe's most democratic constitutions.

Peter Christen Asbjørnsen (1812–1885)

Together with the clergyman Jørgen Moe (1813–1882) he collected and wrote down folk tales and legends. Th language of these tales was remarkabl for the Norwegianness of its vocabulary and sentence structure.

Ivar Aasen (1812–1896)

A farmer's son from the Sunnmøre district of western Norway, Aasen objected strongly to the fact that ordinary Norwegians had to write Danish. He decided to create a written Norwegian language based on the spoken language. For four years he travelled around the country researching the spoken language. His written language is now known as New Norwegian.

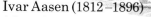

Rana
Kristiansund — Trondheim
Molde
Ålesund
Bergen
Kristiania (Oslo)
Stavanger
Kristiansand

The trolls in the folk tales were wealthy, a could obtain power o human beings – prefe ably beautiful princes Fortunately the troll were also stupid and easily to trick.

The 1820s and 1830s	1840s	1850s
The illustration shows Henrik Wergeland (1808–1845). He was a Romantic, devoted to Norway and the Norwegian landscape, and one of the country's most prolific lyricists. He was also an educationalist and a keen user of a more Norwegian form of language. He worked tirelessly to open Norway's borders to Jews. They acquired that right only in 1851, six years after his death. Wergeland is little known in other countries though he ranks as one of Norway's greatest poets.	In the 1840s many collectors of folk songs, folk tales and folk music were active. The drawing shows a talented folk musician, Myllarguten, who imparted a lot of his knowledge to the famous violinist Ole Bull. At this time, too, artists discovered Norway as a source of motifs, and some of the best-known paintings of Norwegian landscape and folk life date from the 1840s. «Birch Tree in a Storm» by J.C.Dahl (Bergen Art Gallery) and «Bridal Journey in Hardanger» by H.Gude and A.Tidemand (Nasjonalgalleriet, Oslo) are good examples.	This decade was a perio transition in Norwegia literature. The nation's life and history were sti interest but authors als became increasingly aw of contemporary proble The bank note (right) sh Camilla Collet, whose n famous novel *The Prefe Daughters* (1859) was a powerful statement of women's rights.

Synnøve and Torbjørn outside the church: a scene from *Synnøve Solbakken*, a short novel by Bjørnstjerne Bjørnson (1857). The story is set in the countryside of his day, but it is no idyll. Bjørnson exposes the struggle between good and evil.

The photograph above shows Ingrid Bergman as Hedda Gabler and Claude Dauphin as Eilert Løvborg in Henrik Ibsen's play of 1890, *Hedda Gabler* (Theatre Montparnasse, Paris, 1962). The character Hedda Gabler is typical of her time: a woman whose talents are unused and who therefore becomes destructive of herself and others. The play dates from Ibsen's last period as playwright.

Ibsen is best known for his plays of the 1870s and 1880s which were critical of contemporary society. He attacked all forms of bourgeois hypocrisy. *A Doll's House* (1879) is particularly famous. It has been interpreted as putting the case for the emancipation of women.

Although Ibsen holds an exceptional position in 19th-century literature, he does not stand alone. From the mid century on, many authors emerged and helped put Norway on the world literary map.

Henrik Ibsen (1828–1906)

(Portrait by Erik Werenskiold) Ibsen is Norway's best known playwright. He suffered many disappointments while working as artistic director in the theatre. He lived abroad for 30 years and became an acknowledged writer both in and outside Norway.

Amalie Skram (1846–1905)

To a greater extent than her male contemporaries, she wrote from personal experience. She produced harrowing descriptions of young and inexperienced women's encounters with marriage and sexuality. For this she was severely criticised. Her later works were about destitution and her experiences as a patient in a mental hospital. All the obstacles she had to face made Amalie Skram at the end of her life wish to be thought of as a Danish author.

Knut Hamsun (1859–1952)

(Drawing by Olaf Gulbransson) He was critical of both earlier and contemporary Norwegian literature. In his first works the principal characters are lonely, nervous men. His disapproval of industrialisation became gradually more pronounced. And from the early 1930s he sympathised with the Nazis in Germany.

1860s	1870–1890
Fascination with the typically Norwegian and with Norwegian history persisted into the 1860s, and both Henrik Ibsen and Bjørnstjerne Bjørnson wrote historical plays. Two of Bjørnson's plays of the 1860s have medieval themes, *King Sverre* and *Sigurd Slembe*. Bjørnson also wrote the words of Norway's national anthem. Yet the most celebrated works of the decade are Ibsen's plays *Brand* and *Peer Gynt*.	This period tends to be labelled «realism» in Norway. The goal of artists was to re-create reality and to provoke discussion of contemporary problems. The role of women in society, the position of the Church, and education were issues frequently treated in literature. The drawing shows Nora dancing the tarantella in A *Doll's House*, probably Henrik Ibsen's best-known play (1879). Around 1890 some authors began to draw on different subjects and write more about the emotional life of the individual than about social problems.

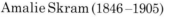

A. Tidemand: «Norwegian Christmas Customs», 1848. The artist was strongly influenced by the national romanticism that characterised much of Norwegian cultural life at that time.

1800–1850: On the Threshold of a New Society

In 1800 the population of Norway was just below 900,000. It increased rapidly throughout the century. In 1865 the figure was 1.7 million, in 1900 2.2 million. Reduced infant mortality was an important factor.

Historians have drawn attention to several causes for the growth in population. People's diet improved, in that herring and potato replaced barley porridge as the staple dish. The war years at the start of the century were a stimulus to potato cultivation, and by 1830 potatoes were described as «the most prized food of the working people». Harvests were dependable, and the nutritional yield of a plot of land might be double that achieved by growing grain there. Herring catches were so plentiful after the turn of the century that herrings became cheap everyday food even in inland areas.

Hygiene improved, too. In the 18th cent-

ury, most houses in south-eastern Norway had acquired a fireplace with a chimney, or a tiled stove. Thus they became cleaner, free of all the soot and grime which had filled them in the days of an old central hearth and a hole in the roof to let out the smoke. By 1850 these improvements had reached the west and north of the country, too.

First signs of the radical changes that came about later in the 19th century are already manifest in the period 1814–1850: pressure of population, emigration, industrialisation.

Rural society managed to absorb the growth in population. New land was cleared for cultivation, a development which required manpower. The number of cottar families continued to increase until it peaked at 67,000 in around 1850. By then some areas were overcrowded. The farmers could afford better implements such as iron ploughs and harrows, and more abundant harvests resulted. However, it would be wrong to speak of a technical revolution in Norwegian agriculture during this period.

At the same time, the towns grew. The population of the capital, Christiania, increased from about 9000 in 1800 to almost 40,000 in 1855. Christiania was changing from a sleepy provincial town to a modern capital, and the Storting authorised the money for buildings which even today are among the capital's principal features: the Royal Palace, the University, the National Hospital, the Bank of Norway.

The earliest emigration to America took place in this period. It began in 1825 with the departure from Stavanger of the sloop «*Restaurationen*» carrying 52 Quakers who were leaving Norway for religious reasons. They settled in the fertile valley of the Fox River in northern Illinois. Over the years, Norwegian colonies were established in the Midwest, and the pioneering efforts of the early settlers eased the way for newcomers. Yet the mass exodus did not start until the 1860s. Between then and 1930, 800,000 Norwegians emigrated to America, and nowadays there are as many people of Norwegian descent in the USA as there are in Norway.

A new type of industry took root in Norway in the 1840s : the textile industry which was quite distinct from the old mines and sawmills of the 18th century. Within a few years, textile mills were built along the River Aker in Christiania and also near Bergen. Some of them had over a hundred employees. The factory owners bought machinery and equipment from England, besides acquiring the necessary expertise there. In this first phase of industrialisation in Norway the textile mills produced for the home market. The machinery needed maintenance, and Norwegians soon decided that they wanted to construct and develop machinery themselves. Thus the first engineering works in the country were established in the 1840s.

At about this time the pressure of population began to be felt in the countryside. Competition for the available work grew keener, and becoming a cottar was difficult. In 1848–9 the country was hit by economic crisis. The mine-owners and timber merchants had problems selling their goods, and this resulted in lower wages and unemployment for foresters, carters and charcoal burners. Against this background the Thranite Movement emerged.

At the turn of the year 1848–9, Marcus Thrane, then a young student, founded the first labour union. It had 160 members.

Growth was rapid. Two years later there were 300 such unions around the country, some 30,000 members in all. These were mainly cottars, workers and artisans, though they included also a few farmers. Leading figures in the world of the arts, the poets Henrik Ibsen and Aasmund Olavsson Vinje for instance, also participated in the movement. The followers of Thrane fought for equality, demanding universal suffrage for men, general conscription, better primary education, and equality before the law. They campaigned, too, for lower prices and in particular the repeal of the import duty on corn. Finally they claimed that the government should make it easier for people to obtain land by giving untilled ground to men who owned none but cleared some for cultivation.

Marcus Thrane had visited London and Paris. He was familiar with the ideas that inspired the February Revolution of 1848, and was of course encouraged by that event. Officials and farmers alike feared Thrane's followers and their talk of revolution, and in 1851 Thrane and other leaders of the movement were arrested. By the time Thrane was freed in 1859 and emigrated to America, the movement he had once led had faded away.

However, even though it was crushed, this first workers' movement heralded a new age. The seeds of change in both town and country were to grow, and mature by the end of the century.

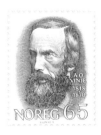

The Head Office of the Bank of Norway was established in Trondheim in 1816. The Christiania Branch got its own building in 1830 (right). The building on the left is the Christiania Theatre. Painting by Chr. M. Grosch, 1836–37.

Emigration

In 1824 Klein Pedersen Hesthammer was sent to the USA by Norwegian Quakers to investigate the possibility of emigration. In America he was given the name Cleng Peerson.

After 1860 emigration to the USA began in earnest. The rapid increase in population in Norway meant that times were hard for many. America seemed very tempting. People had heard about fantastic wages and cheap farm land. In 1862 the American Congress passed the Homestead Act which granted new settlers up to 160 acres of land to farm. Friends and relatives wrote letters from America, praising their new country.

Emigration took place in phases. When the last great wave was over, more than 800,000 had crossed the Atlantic. Only Ireland had a higher emigration rate in relation to the total population. Mainly young people emigrated, the majority of them men. Until 1880 whole families would set off together. Later it was mainly single men and women. Most did well in their new home, though there were some who died during the sea-crossing, came to sad ends in the slums of big cities, or were killed by Indians. Nowadays there is hardly a Norwegian family without relatives in the USA.

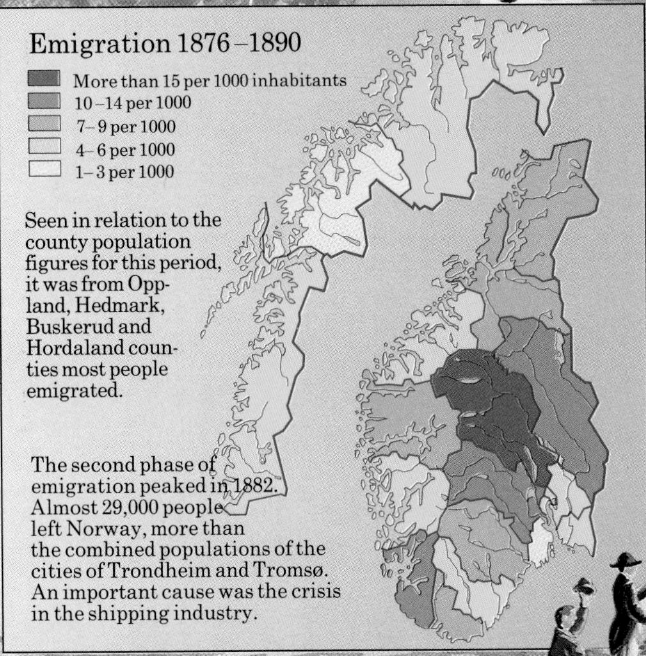

Emigration 1876–1890

- More than 15 per 1000 inhabitants
- 10–14 per 1000
- 7–9 per 1000
- 4–6 per 1000
- 1–3 per 1000

Seen in relation to the county population figures for this period, it was from Oppland, Hedmark, Buskerud and Hordaland counties most people emigrated.

The second phase of emigration peaked in 1882. Almost 29,000 people left Norway, more than the combined populations of the cities of Trondheim and Tromsø. An important cause was the crisis in the shipping industry.

The sloop «Restaurationen» sailed from Stavanger in 1825 with 52 emigrants on board. They were Quakers and wished to practise their religion unmolested. They settled in the Fox River valley in Illinois.

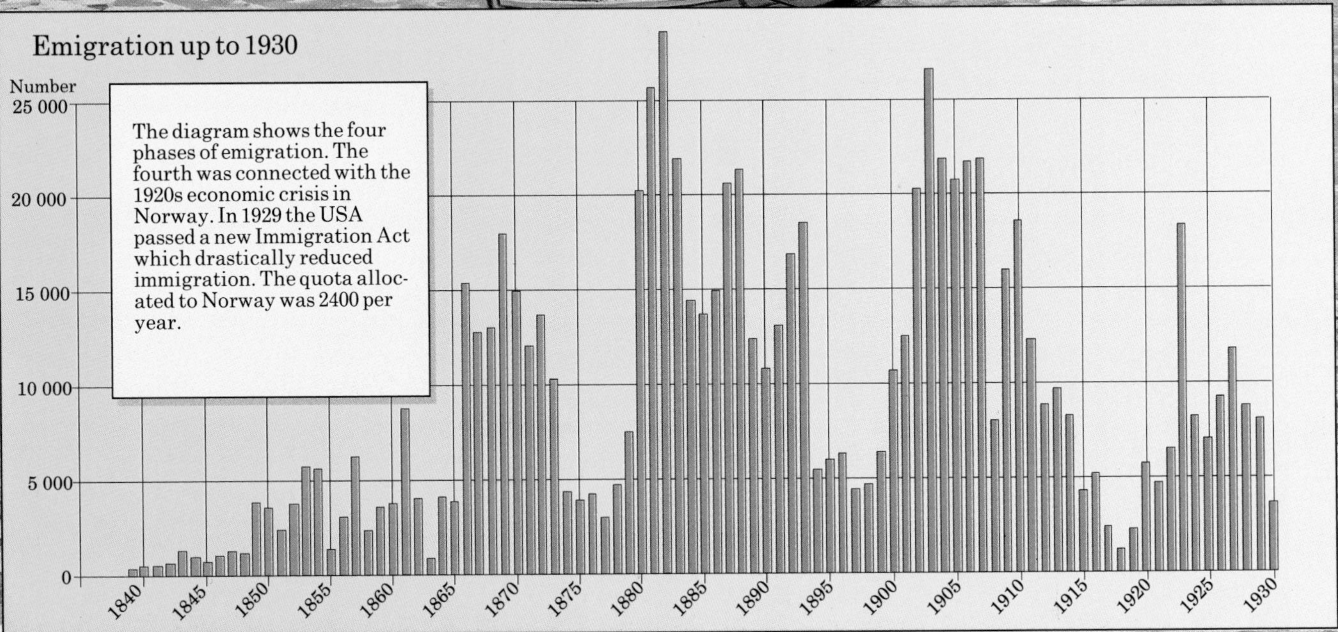

Emigration up to 1930

Number

The diagram shows the four phases of emigration. The fourth was connected with the 1920s economic crisis in Norway. In 1929 the USA passed a new Immigration Act which drastically reduced immigration. The quota allocated to Norway was 2400 per year.

25 000
20 000
15 000
10 000
5 000
0

1840 1845 1850 1855 1860 1865 1870 1875 1880 1885 1890 1895 1900 1905 1910 1915 1920 1925 1930

Farmers of Norwegian descent harvesting wheat in Kosh-konong, Wisconsin, c.1875. The photographer was Andrew Dahl (1844–1923).

This map shows where most of the immigrants of Norwegian origin settled prior to 1910. The majority had been attracted to the states of the Midwest, west of the Great Lakes. Nowadays Norwegian place-names abound in these rich agricultural areas. But the states of the north west were also popular with Norwegians.

The figures on the map represent persons born in Norway or born in the USA to Norwegian parents.

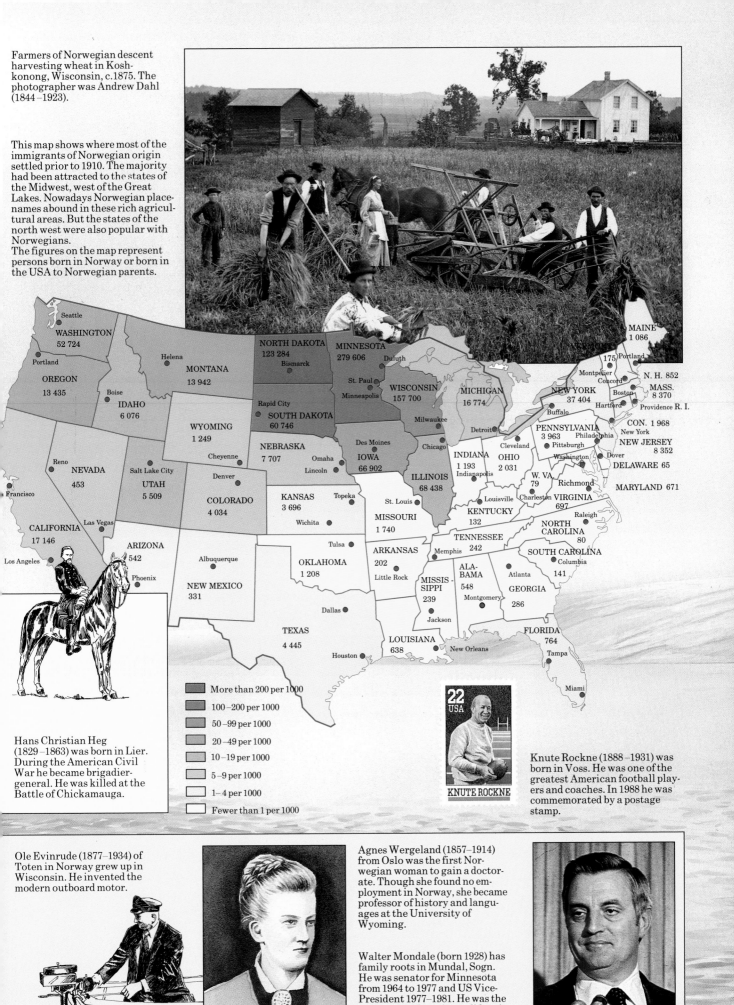

Seattle
WASHINGTON
52 724
Portland
OREGON
13 435
Helena
MONTANA
13 942
Bismarck
NORTH DAKOTA
123 284
MINNESOTA
279 606
Duluth
St. Paul
Minneapolis
WISCONSIN
157 700
MICHIGAN
16 774
Detroit
Milwaukee
Chicago
MAINE
1 086
175 Portland
Montpelier
Concord
N. H. 852
Boston
MASS.
8 370
Hartford
Providence R. I.
NEW YORK
37 404
Buffalo
CON. 1 968
New York
NEW JERSEY
8 352
Boise
IDAHO
6 076
Rapid City
SOUTH DAKOTA
60 746
WYOMING
1 249
Cheyenne
NEBRASKA
7 707
Omaha
Lincoln
Des Moines
IOWA
66 902
ILLINOIS
68 438
St. Louis
INDIANA
1 193
Indianapolis
OHIO
2 031
Cleveland
Pittsburgh
PENNSYLVANIA
3 963
Philadelphia
Washington
Dover
DELAWARE 65
MARYLAND 671
W. VA
79
Richmond
Reno
NEVADA
453
Salt Lake City
UTAH
5 509
Denver
COLORADO
4 034
KANSAS
3 696
Topeka
Wichita
MISSOURI
1 740
KENTUCKY
132
Louisville
Charleston
VIRGINIA
697
Raleigh
NORTH
CAROLINA
80
Francisco
CALIFORNIA
17 146
Las Vegas
ARIZONA
542
Albuquerque
Los Angeles
Phoenix
NEW MEXICO
331
OKLAHOMA
1 208
Tulsa
ARKANSAS
202
Little Rock
Memphis
TENNESSEE
242
SOUTH CAROLINA
Columbia
141
MISSIS-
SIPPI
239
Jackson
ALA-
BAMA
548
Montgomery
GEORGIA
286
Atlanta
Dallas
TEXAS
4 445
Houston
LOUISIANA
638
New Orleans
FLORIDA
764
Tampa
Miami

More than 200 per 1000
100–200 per 1000
50–99 per 1000
20–49 per 1000
10–19 per 1000
5–9 per 1000
1–4 per 1000
Fewer than 1 per 1000

Hans Christian Heg (1829–1863) was born in Lier. During the American Civil War he became brigadier-general. He was killed at the Battle of Chickamauga.

22 USA
KNUTE ROCKNE

Knute Rockne (1888–1931) was born in Voss. He was one of the greatest American football players and coaches. In 1988 he was commemorated by a postage stamp.

Ole Evinrude (1877–1934) of Toten in Norway grew up in Wisconsin. He invented the modern outboard motor.

Agnes Wergeland (1857–1914) from Oslo was the first Norwegian woman to gain a doctorate. Though she found no employment in Norway, she became professor of history and languages at the University of Wyoming.

Walter Mondale (born 1928) has family roots in Mundal, Sogn. He was senator for Minnesota from 1964 to 1977 and US Vice-President 1977–1981. He was the Democratic Party's candidate in the presidential election of 1984, but did not win.

Towards an Industrial Society

It is impossible to understand the rapid development in the second half of the 19th century without casting a glance beyond Norway's frontiers. The whole of Europe was undergoing change. Germany and Italy were unified into populous nation states, and industrialisation proceeded apace. Railways improved communication all over the continent. Consequently demand for goods and services grew, also from little Norway on Europe's fringe. The Norwegian economy became more closely tied to other countries, for better and for worse. Norway became more prosperous, but also more at the mercy of international economic cycles. Large sections of the population went over to a money economy.

In the 1840s and 50s the Storting passed several laws which facilitated internal trade. Anyone who wished could set up in a trade in town or country; a country shopkeeper no longer needed to be a citizen of a town; anyone who wished could run a sawmill. A trade policy of this kind was in line with the liberalism then prevailing in Europe, and the Storting also resolved to remove many of the country's protective import duties. Trade should flow as freely as possible across frontiers.

Roads were built at a great pace, and within 50 years the total length of Norway's roads was doubled. Steamships plied regular routes along the coast and on the principal lakes. And in 1854 the country's first railway, from Christiania to Eidsvoll, was opened. Its main cargo was timber, carried from Lake Øyeren to Christiania, though agricultural produce was also transported. The capital was expanding rapidly and needed supplies of fresh foods from the surrounding districts. There followed fifty years of railway building. In 1910, three quarters of the present-day railway network had been completed. In 1855 the first telegraph line came into operation, and soon telegraph wires crisscrossed the country. In 1880 Norway's first telephone line was opened in the presence of the inventor himself, Graham Bell. At the turn of the century there were 24,000 telephones in Norway. The postal services were made less complicated, too, in that postage rates became the same for the whole country.

The steamship «Ganger Rolf» of Christiania was built in 1856. Steamships still had sails because the steam engines were unable to utilise fully the energy from coal. Painting by W. D. Penny, 1857.

J. Flintoe: Old hostelry
in Maridalsveien,
Christiania, about
1830. In the early nin-
teenth century the aver-
age Norwegian drank
about 16 litres of pure
alcohol a year. In the
1980s average con-
sumption was one third
of this amount.

In the period 1850–1880, Norwegian shipping experienced its third «golden age». The merchant fleet increased in size from 300,000 to 1.5 million net registered tons. Larger vessels came into use, and 60,000 seamen were employed on Norwegian ships in around 1880. By then Norway had the third largest merchant fleet in the world, after Great Britain and the USA.

There were several reasons for this Norwegian success. World trade increased by over 50 % each decade from 1840 to 1870, and the obvious way to transport goods was by sea. Great Britain with its large population was Norway's principal trading partner, and the British were dependent on seaborne supplies. After the repeal of the Navigation Act in 1850, ships of all nationalities could freely carry goods to Britain, and the Norwegians seized their opportunity. Norway had a long tradition of shipping, and in coastal regions there were qualified seamen just waiting to sign on. Wages were low, and many ships were in a wretched condition. Sailors joked that if a ship was carrying timber,

the cargo would keep it afloat if anything went wrong. And that happened frequently. Some years more than one ship in ten went down.

Whereas Norwegian ships around 1850 plied mainly in European waters and carried mainly timber, long-distance voyages played a larger role from the 1860s on. Norwegian ships began serving ports in the USA, Africa, South America, China, India and Australia, and their varied cargoes included rice, coffee, sugar, cotton, coal, ice and tropical fruits. Nevertheless, in the mid-1870s half of the total volume carried was still timber.

Joint ownership was the most common form of shipowning, with several people owning a share of a ship. The majority were merchants, but farmers, timber traders, shipbuilders, sailmakers, captains, ship's mates and ordinary seamen could also be shareholders. Frequently those who contributed materials or labour to a ship were repaid not in money but with shares. Women, too, are known to have owned shares. Shareholding ownership has been called ownership by the people, which is of course an exaggeration, but the system did help finance a shipping boom in a country with only rudimentary financial institutions. Furthermore, shareholders worked closely with shipbuilders, whose small yards lay scattered along the coast; there were very few large yards. And the coastal population learned about the construction and equipping of ships. The shipyards employed large numbers of men, while sailmakers depended on female labour.

Towards the end of the 1870s Norwegian shipping began to stagnate. During the next decade the number of seamen fell by 20,000. Historians disagree as to the causes of the crisis. Perhaps the Norwegians were overtaken by other seafaring nations because they changed from sail to steam too slowly? Some maintain that Norwegian shipowners were conservative, and clung to their white sails. Others find the explanation in the country's lack of capital, given that a steamship cost five times

as much as a sailing ship of the same carrying capacity. Nevertheless some shipowners did buy steamships in the 1890s. The age of joint ownership was over, as was the age of sail.

A new phase in the industrialisation of Norway began in the 1860s, with the establishment of an industry which, unlike the textile industry, produced for the export market. Steam engines were introduced to drive the sawmills, and planing mills were founded. In 1863 came the first pulp mill which manufactured paper, the Bentse Works at Sagene (the latter name means «the sawmills»), a suburb of Christiania. In time, the pulp mills acquired water-turbines which made the machinery more powerful. In 1890 Norway had 60 pulp mills, profitable concerns even during the economic depression of the 1880s. The first cellulose factory in Norway, Hafslunds Chemiske Trævarefabrik near Sarpsborg, began operation in 1874. Planing machines and turbines were manufactured at the fast expanding engineering works. Myren's Works in Christiania was particularly progressive and supplied equipment to both Swedish and Finnish planing mills.

The new industries required a lot of capital, and much of that came from abroad, particularly from England. Norway's natural resources and cheap labour attracted foreign investors. The commercial banks which had been founded in Norway around 1850 also raised valuable capital for Norwegian industry. At the turn of the century, manufacturing industry accounted for 28 % of the gross national product, and employed over a quarter of the country's active work force.

People flocked from the countryside to the towns and villages in search of work. In 1870, about 20 % of the population lived in towns and built-up areas; by the turn of the century the figure was well over 30 %. The population of Christiania increased from 75,000 in 1870 to 230,000 in 1900. And Bergen and Trondheim were like regional capitals, with 72,000 and 38,000 inhabitants respectively in 1900.

The industrial workers' day was long, often between 10 and 12 hours, and monotonous. Many of them worked additional hours, and there was no annual holiday. Uncovered cog wheels and driving belts on cold premises made their places of work both dangerous and unhealthy. The first legislation on the protection of workers came only in the 1890s. Men and women received different pay even if they did the same job: a woman, not being the family breadwinner, got half a man's wage. Child labour was widespread. It was cheap, and families could not manage without the children's earnings.

It was in the tobacco and match industries that half the labour force consisted of boys and girls under 15 years of age. Of all industrial workers in 1875 almost 10% were children under 15. Not until 1892 was legislation enacted to fix the lower age limit for child labour at 12 years. Young people under the age of 18 were permitted to work «only» 10 hours a day.

In the early years of industrialisation, shanty towns grew up around the new factories. Later, well-to-do citizens built large tenement blocks where many worker families were housed in small flats. The owners of these properties reaped considerable profits, but at the same time the crowded living conditions created a sense of cohesion among the workers. In the Grunerløkka area of Oslo the tenement blocks still stand, preserving the memory of the 19th-century industrial workers.

Far from the noise and smoke of the factories the bourgeoisie lived in detached villas and grand apartments, with servants to take care of the housework and the children. In the towns, class distinctions were marked, and even though their standard of living was not lower than that of cotters and servants, many industrial workers felt that they should have a bigger share of the wealth created by industry.

Workers at Mesna Bruk in Lillehammer in the 1890s. On the left, Børsum's famous horse-drawn rake; on the right, a two-horse reaper. Mr. Børsum himself is in the middle with all the medals won by the company.

Industrialisation

New manufacturing industries arrived from Great Britain in the 1840s. The first textile mills were built in Christiania and near Bergen and Trondheim. Engineering workshops made their appearance at about the same date. In the 1860s and 70s came pulp mills and cellulose factories.

A third phase of industrialisation opened after 1900. The power of waterfalls was harnessed, and the factories began using electricity. New roads were built, and railway, steamer, postal and telegraphic services linked the different parts of the country. Between 1865 and 1900 the urban population increased from 15 % to 30 % of the total population. In 1900 manufacturing industry accounted for 28 % of the gross national product and employed over a quarter of the country's active labour force.

Røros copper works exemplifies the old type of industry in Norway. This 18th-century painting by Mathias Dalager shows the smelting works with Røros church in the background.

The engineering works Trondhjems Mekaniske Verksted A/S dates from 1843. It produced the first Norwegian-built locomotive «Thrønderen» in 1861.

The textile factory Hjula Veveri on the river Aker in Christiania was established in 1849. On this 1866 view by Carl Baagøe it is seen to the left of the waterfall. To the right is the paper mill Nedre Papirmølle. The weaver (right) at the Hjula mill was painted in 1887–8 by Wilhelm Peters; the picture was commissioned by the factory owner. Most of the workers in the textile industry were women.

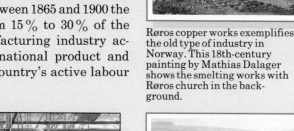

Norway's first railway went from Christiania to Eidsvoll and was opened in 1854.

Norway's first telegraph line, between Christiania and Drammen, came into operation in 1855. By 1871 telegraph wires extended as far as Kirkenes in Finnmark county. The first Norwegian postage stamp was issued in 1854, when the same postal rates were applied to the entire country. The postal and telegraphic services provided employment for many women.

Borregaard fabriker, Sarpsborg

The cellulose and paper factories at Borregaard near Sarpsborg were built for a British company in the 1890s. In 1905 this enterprise was Norway's largest with about 1000 employees.

The turn-of-the-century photograph below shows women workers in a canning factory in Stavanger. The «Man with the Fish» sardine-tin label was designed by Theodor Kittelsen in 1905.

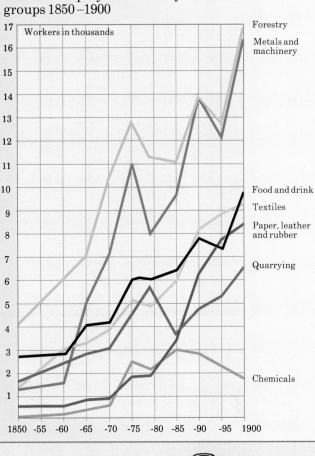

Workers employed in the major industrial groups 1850–1900

Workers in thousands

Forestry

Metals and machinery

Food and drink

Textiles

Paper, leather and rubber

Quarrying

Chemicals

1850 -55 -60 -65 -70 -75 -80 -85 -90 -95 1900

FINEST NORWEGIAN
Sardines
in OLIVE OIL
Net weight
3½ oz.
CHR. BJELLAND & Co.
STAVANGER
GRAND PRIX & DIPLOMAS OF HONOR 20 GOLDMEDALS

In 1899 several trade unions wishing to unite in the struggle for better pay and working conditions formed what today is the Norwegian Federation of Trade Unions. In response, the Norwegian Employers' Confederation was founded the following year. Not until 1935 did the two bodies sign an agreement which regulated relations between employers and employees.

AFL

NAF

Many of the navvies who built the railways moved from one construction site to another. A good number of them were Swedes. The illustration shows a Mayday demonstration for shorter working hours. The claim for an eight hour working day in industry was not met until 1919.

8
Timers
arbeidsdag

A Revolution in Agriculture

Around 1850 the majority of farms were self-sufficient. Spinning wheels and looms were put to good use. Farmers forged their own implements in smithies on the farm, and in the forest they gathered the materials for their wooden tools and for domestic utensils. Women made cheese, churned butter, and distilled spirits. However, fifty years later, in almost all parts of the country, agricultural goods were being produced for sale. New equipment had made farming more efficient and reduced the need for crofters and labourers. Thousands had moved to the towns or emigrated to America. Change came first to the rural districts on railway routes or near towns.

The growth of the towns ensured ever larger markets for the farmers, but this meant of course that they had to increase their output. As a result many of them introduced both rotation of crops and artificial fertilisers. Good iron ploughs produced bigger yields, and horse-drawn rakes, seed drills, and reaping and threshing machines all reduced the need for labour. Use of such equipment increased dramatically towards the end of the century: in 1875 there were 1300 reaping machines in Norway; twenty five years later 30,000. Cattle were better fed and cared for and gave more milk, and in areas where strip farming was practised the authorities arranged exchanges of land so that each farmer acquired a single sizeable plot to cultivate, and farms could be run more efficiently.

Milk, butter and cheese gave the greatest profits. The produce was sent to the towns, and the farmers were paid in cash. More and more of them went over to dairy farming and began buying imported corn. Corn from the USA and Russia was cheap, and was brought to Norway by steamship and rail. Gradually, making butter and cheese on the farm ceased to be so profitable and from the 1870s farmers cooperated to build dairies. In 1875 there were 100 in Norway, mainly in the south-east, but as yet their output was only a small frac-

tion of the total production up and down the country.

The Breakdown of Government by State Officials

In the 1860s the association called «Friends of the Farmers» was founded by farmer and Storting member Søren Jaabæk. About 25,000 joined the association which helped bring about the election of more farmers to the Storting. From 1868 they were in the majority. The «Friends of the Farmers» were anxious that central and local government should economise, and not spend money fostering new trade and industry. The farmers felt that the burden of taxation weighed too heavily on them: municipal taxes were twice as high in 1870 as they had been in 1850.

The Cabinet was the farmers' chief adversary. Holders of public office still dominated the political scene, and the climax of a politician's career was appointment as one of the king's ministers. Jaabæk and the farmers allied themselves with Johan Sverdrup, a member of the Storting who headed a group of radical academics, and together they aimed at diminishing the power of the public officials. Sverdrup believed that the Storting should lead the way. *«All power in this chamber»*, he declared. The majority in the Storting wished to control the Cabinet, which they felt should be responsible to the national assembly.

From there developments moved fast. As early as in 1869 the Storting voted to assemble every year. Thus greater control could be exercised over the Government. In 1872 the Storting adopted an amendment to the Constitution obliging ministers to appear before the Storting and defend their policies. The idea was to draw them out of the gloom of their rooms at the ministries. However, the King refused to approve this, pointing out that the theory of the separation of powers underlay the entire Constitution. Sverdrup and the farmers maintained that the King had no right of veto in matters concerning the

Constitution, and the legislation was in fact passed by three consecutive sessions of the Storting. The Cabinet continued to advise the King not to give his assent. There was deadlock.

The opposition farmers in the Storting decided to impeach the Government before a special court known as the *Riksrett,* where members of the *Lagting* sit in judgement together with the High Court judges, while the *Odelsting* prosecutes. After the 1882 election, Sverdrup's supporters, who by then were known as *Venstre* (the Left), had 83 out of 114 seats in the Storting. Several ministers headed by Prime Minister Christian August Selmer were sentenced to loss of office, others to fines. The court decided that the Cabinet had been wrong to advise the King to withhold his assent from the constitutional amendment concerning ministers.

In great secrecy King Oscar II made plans for a coup, but they were never implemented. In June 1884 he asked Johan Sverdrup, the leader of the majority in the Storting, to form a government. This was the first time a politician became Prime Minister because he had a majority of the members of the national assembly behind him: parliamentarism had been introduced in Norway, and the officials' firm grip on government was loosened. Future governments would come and go according to the relative strength of groups within the Storting.

The conflict about ministerial responsibility and the king's right of veto led to the forming of the Liberal and Conservative Parties (*Venstre* and *Høyre,* the Left and the Right respectively). The Liberals were supported mainly by the farmers but also by teachers and salaried employees. During the 1880s the Liberal Party managed to put into effect many of its main policies. A new Suffrage Act gave about one half of the male electorate the vote, though it was not until 1898 that universal suffrage for men was introduced. The New Norwegian language was put on a par with Dano-Norwegian, and the country acquired two – fairly similar – official written languages. A Criminal Procedure Act laid down that a jury of laymen should determine the question of guilt in criminal cases. The

Drawing of a session of the impeachment trial, February 1884. The main accused, Prime Minister Selmer, is seated alone in the background on the left.

Sven Jørgensen:
«Unemployed», 1888.

Education Acts of 1889 introduced seven years' compulsory schooling for all children. However, not everything went smoothly for Sverdrup. A Government proposal to pay a stipend to the author and social critic Alexander Kielland led to a split in the Liberal Party. The Conservative Party, backed by the public officials and the merchant class, came to power in 1889.

In society at large, people were forming alliances. During the 1880s and 1890s it became increasingly usual for both men and women workers to organise in trade unions. Conflicts with employers showed the need for solidarity in the struggle for improved working conditions and better pay. Within the same trade, local unions formed a nation-wide trade union, and in 1899 these unions together established the Norwegian Federation of Trade Unions. Among its other functions was advising members on all trade union matters. The following year the Norwegian Employers' Confederation was founded, in response to the growing threat from unionised labour. The Norwegian Labour Party was formed in 1887. It soon adopted socialism and demanded shorter working hours and the vote for all men and women. Yet at first it did not attract much support, as many workers voted for the Liberals. In 1903, the Labour Party won four seats in the Storting, three of the members coming from the county of Troms, where fisheries provided the main means of livelihood.

During the final decades of the 19th century, the struggle for equality of the sexes was an important issue. New opportunities for women, particularly for middle class women, were opening up. Women were now admitted to middle and grammar schools; and primary schools as well as the postal and telegraph services were in need of qualified labour. In 1884 women won the right to sit all the final examinations at the University, but it was some time before many applied, and employment opportunities were few. Several leading figures spoke out on behalf of women's emancipation, and the plays of Henrik Ibsen provoked debate on the subject. Both men and women joined the Norwegian League of Feminists when it was founded in 1884. And the following year saw the establishment of the Norwegian Women's Suffrage Union. However, their demands met with opposition in and outside the Storting. Women's work was in the home, it was said; women were fickle, and unsuitable for positions of responsibility. Yet women took bastion after bastion. At first only women above a

certain income were enfranchised, but in 1913 the Storting extended to all women the right to vote at elections. In 1924 the first woman won a seat in the Storting.

Christian Krohg: «Albertine in the Police Doctor's Waiting Room», 1886–87. Prostitution was widespread in the largest Norwegian towns in the nineteenth century.

Theodor Kittelsen's «Strike» is the first Norwegian painting with a clear social message. The earliest sketch for the painting was made in 1877.

Norwegian soldiers sharpening their swords in connection with the dissolution of the union in 1905.

Edvard Grieg (1843–1907) is unchallenged as Norway's greatest composer. There are many elements of Norwegian folk music in Grieg's compositions, which have won international acclaim.

The Dissolution of the Union with Sweden in 1905

Ever since 1814, Norway had been the junior partner in the union, and towards the end of the 19th century dissension flared up. Many believed that the economic significance of union for Norway was dwindling, and indeed in 1895 the Swedes terminated the free trade agreement between the two realms. A further cause of tension was Swedish foreign policy. King Oscar II declared that Germany was and ought to be «*our closest and most natural ally*», whereas Norwegians felt their ties were with Great Britain. They also objected to having a Swedish foreign minister and joint consular representation abroad. Only purely Norwegian consulates, they held, could safeguard the inte-

rests of the country's trade and industry.

During the 1890s the Liberal Party took the lead in trying to solve the foreign affairs dispute. It declared that Norway should have her own foreign minister, and that a solely Norwegian consular service was a minimum requirement. The Conservative Party supported the latter demand but insisted on negotiations with the Swedes. In 1895 the Liberal Party was forced to accept such negotiations because the Swedes threatened war. In the following years the two parties alternated in power, and eventually the negotiations were put in cold storage. However, during this period the Storting allocated more funds to defence.

On the initiative of the Swedes, fresh negotiations regarding consular representation started. It was agreed that Norway should have her own consuls and the Swedes should propose the necessary legislation. This agreement led to another split in the Liberal Party. Radical members of the party felt that it would prevent Norway acquiring a fully independent foreign service. But the moderates, led by shipowner and Storting member Christian Michelsen, broke away and fought the ensuing election together with the Conservatives as the Unity Party. Their slogan was devised by the writer Bjørnstjerne Bjørnson, «We know no way but that of negotiation!»

The Unity Party won the election in 1903, and the Swedes put forward their legislation on consular representation. Norway was to have her own consuls, but the foreign minister would continue to be Swedish and the Norwegian consuls would be subordinate to him. This was unacceptable to the Norwegians, and the political parties prepared for battle under the banner «Out of the Union!» Christian Michelsen became Prime Minister in a broad-based coalition government which only the Labour Party did not join.

In the spring of 1905, legislation establishing a Norwegian consular service was passed by the Storting, and when the King refused to give his assent, the

Government resigned. On 7 June the Storting voted unanimously that «the union with Sweden under one King has ceased to exist, as a consequence of the King having ceased to function as King of Norway». The principal argument was that he had failed to provide the country with a new Government.

The resolution of 7 June caused consternation in Sweden, and conservative elements wanted to resort to war. Norwegian troops were ordered out to the border, but fortunately the more moderate views prevailed in Sweden and there were new negotiations. The Storting tried to appease the Swedes by offering the Norwegian throne to a prince of the Swedish royal family, but the offer was rejected. In August a plebiscite on the union was held. A mere 184 male voters were in favour of continued union, while women collected 250,000 signatures in support of its dissolution. After a tough round of negotiations in the autumn, Norway agreed to dismantle most of the border fortifications.

One problem remained. Should Norway continue to be a monarchy? The Government decided it should, and offered the throne to Prince Carl of Denmark. Carl was married to Princess Maud, daughter of the British King, and they had a two year old son. The Prince asked that the Norwegian people should express their

After 1850 people began to join organisations and the missionary societies attracted a lot of support. Missionary work was independent of the Church of Norway, but the missionary organisations cooperated with the Church and the clergy. The first missionary society in Norway was the Norwegian Missionary Society, founded in 1842. The Overseas Mission was active in Madagascar and through its newspaper, Norsk Misjonstidende, the society provided information about conditions in Madagascar and other foreign countries, while at the same time encouraging people to support the work of the mission. In the 1840s and 1850s many local societies were established all over the country. The work of the Home Mission started in the 1850s and became a national organisation under the Norwegian Lutheran Foundation in 1868. Its purpose was to foster pietistic, «true» Christianity in Norway and the organisation gained great influence over the Church and Norwegian society. The illustration shows Johan Smith teaching in Bara village, Madagascar, c. 1895.

opinion by plebiscite: 80 % voted in favour of monarchy.

The King took the style Haakon VII and gave his son the name Olav. In picking a royal family with close ties in Denmark and Britain, Norway had chosen wisely.

Alt for Norge!

King Haakon VII with Crown Prince Olav on his arm is welcomed by Prime Minister Christian Michelsen in 1905.

The Royal Palace in Oslo is at the western end of Karl Johans gate, the main street of the capital.

In 1905 the people of Norway chose Prince Carl of Denmark as their king. He was married to Princess Maud of England and they had a two-year-old son. Prince Carl took the style Haakon VII and the Crown Prince was given the name Olav. In 1929 Crown Prince Olav married Princess Märtha of Sweden. They had three children, Ragnhild, Astrid and Harald. King Haakon died in 1957 and the Crown Prince came to the throne as King Olav V. On the death of King Olav in 1991 the Crown Prince became King Harald V. In 1968 he had married Sonja Haraldsen of Oslo, and she now became Queen. The King and Queen have two children, Märtha Louise and Haakon Magnus. All three kings adopted the motto «All for Norway».

The king is the country's head of state. Once a week he presides over a formal meeting of the Cabinet. The photograph shows the third Government of Mrs Gro Harlem Brundtland (1990-). In January 1991 King Harald took the oath before the Storting and undertook to rule Norway in accordance with the Constitution. At his side is Queen Sonja.

King Olav on a 1975 state visit in the USA.

King Haakon's coronation in Trondheim, 1906

Queen Maud (1869–1938)

Crown Prince Olav ski jumping, 1923

Crown Prince Olav during the Liberation, 1945

The Norwegian royal family have always been keen on outdoor life and sport. The photograph shows King Haakon, Queen Maud and Crown Prince Olav skiing, c.1910.

Crown Princess Sonja with Queen Margrethe of Denmark skiing in the Rondane Mountains, 1990.

There have been very enthusiastic yachtsmen in the royal family. At the 1928 Summer Olympics Crown Prince Olav won a gold medal in the 6-meter class. On several occasions Crown Prince Harald represented Norway in the Olympics and in World Championships with considerable success. In 1988 in *«Fram X»* he won the one-ton class World Championship. From 1965 to 1969 he was Commodore of the Royal Norwegian Yacht Club.

King Olav soon became a very popular king. He travelled about the country to gain first-hand experience of his people.

During the oil crisis of the mid-1970s there was petrol rationing and even the King used public transport. The photograph shows King Olav in a tram on his way to ski in Oslo's Nordmarka forest.

The royal family on the balcony of the Royal Palace on 17 May, Constitution Day, in 1989. Left to right: Prince Haakon Magnus, Crown Princess Sonja, King Olav, Princess Märtha Louise and Crown Prince Harald.

The National Aid Fund for War Victims

Crown Princess Märtha (1901–1954)

King Olav's consecration in 1958

King Olav sailing

King Olav in dress uniform

King Olav judging ski jumping

NORWAY
AS A FREE
COUNTRY

In a speech after the dissolution of the union, Prime Minister Michelsen said that «a new working day» had begun for Norway, and he was right. The period after 1905 was marked by great changes in a short time. Norway benefited from international economic growth. The population of the towns increased, leading to bigger markets and higher prices for the farmers. The development of communications continued and hydro-electric power from the waterfalls brought electricity to more homes. Electric tramcars were introduced in the largest cities, the first motor vessels hinted of a coming revolution in the fishing and merchant fleets and the first motor cars drove on Norwegian roads.

The political parties soon forgot the union debate and focussed their attention on two main themes – legislation to control the ownership of Norwegian assets, known as the «Concession Laws», and social policy.

Around the turn of the century, Norwegian and foreign capitalists had bought a large number of waterfalls in Norway. The farmers who owned the waterfalls were eager to sell. They needed money to invest in their farms or to emigrate to America. They did not realise how valuable a waterfall could be. One half of the Rjukan falls was bought for NOK 600; the original bid had been only NOK 50. In 1906, three quarters of the waterfalls that had been harnessed to produce hydro-electric power were owned by foreigners and this led to some concern. Who should own Norway's waterfalls, mines and forests? Should the State determine the rate of development?

Many people believed that the State should impose conditions on company owners. Adjacent municipalities should be entitled to cheap electric power and the workers should have good housing. The State should ensure that it received tax revenues and the developers should use Norwegian goods and services. This led to dissent in the Storting but the result was that both Norwegian and foreign compa-

nies had to apply for a licence before they were allowed to start production. With this leverage, the State was able to impose conditions on the developers, and the law laid down that waterfalls with dams should become State property after 60–80 years. Foreigners were not allowed to buy forests at all. It is possible that the Concession Laws slowed the rate of growth of the Norwegian economy but the government ensured national control of the country's natural resources.

Industrialisation did not lead to welfare for all. Many people in the towns felt insecure and missed the old community spirit of rural society. Unemployment, alcoholism, prostitution and homelessness were rife in the working-class districts. The Labour Party and the trade union movement demanded improvements in working conditions, and many in the Liberal Party also believed that the State had a duty to protect the weakest citizens and improve conditions for the workers. The Storting therefore introduced a number of reforms in the period before the First World War. These included sick pay, factory inspection, the Workers Protection Act and the 10-hour day. The 8-hour day for industrial workers was not introduced until 1919. In the same year 115,000 industrial workers gained the legal right to one week's paid holiday a year.

Opposite page: The harnessing of waterfalls inspired many artists. This painting is from Theodor Kittelsen's Rjukan series, 1908–09, and radiates optimism about the future. Man has succeeded in taming the forces of nature!

The first motor-cars aroused great interest. Here two youngsters from Setesdal have dressed up in their best clothes to have their picture taken by famous photographer A. B. Wilse.

Norsk Hydro

In 1905 Sam Eyde founded Norsk Hydro with Swedish, French and Norwegian backing. Together with Kristian Birkeland he had invented an electric arc furnace which produced saltpetre (nitrate) from the nitrogen in the air. The first factory to produce this fertilizer was established in Notodden. The production process required large quantities of electric power, so the company built power

Kristian Birkeland and his assistant by the electric arc furnace

In the first two years artificial fertilizer was packed in barrels.

stations on several waterfalls in Telemark. In 1911 a new fertilizer factory was opened in Rjukan.

In 1927 Norsk Hydro introduced a new method for producing artificial fertilizer from ammonia and built a factory at Porsgrunn. Production of fertilizer containing several other nutrients commenced nine years later.

After the Second World War, Norsk Hydro started to produce other products. At the beginning of the 1950s the company opened the Porsgrunn factories, which manufactured magnesium and PVC, a raw material for plastic production. Ten years later an aluminium smelting works was established on Karmøy. At about the same time the company became involved in oil exploration in the North Sea and production on the Ekofisk field began in 1971. In the 1970s and 1980s the company bought fertilizer factories and aluminium plants abroad and build a petrochemical plant at Rafnes in Bamble. The marketing and refining of oil and gas became increasingly important in the 1980s. At the end of the 1980s, Hydro acquired interests in the pharmaceutical industry and in aquaculture. In 1989 Norsk Hydro had nearly 33,000 employees, of whom approximately half worked in Norway.

Såheim power station provided power for the saltpetre factory five kilometres further down the valley. The town of Rjukan grew up round the factory.

This labourer represents the thousands of men and women who contributed towards building the Rjukan community.

Head Office

○ Sales office

△ Operations office

▽ Research office

☐ Production plant

■ Oil

■ Agriculture

■ Aluminium

■ Petrochemicals

■ Magnesium

■ Biomedicines

■ Ind. chemistry

Light metals

Norsk Hydro produces magnesium in Porsgrunn and in Bécancour, Quebec, Canada, and is one of the largest magnesium producers in the world. Magnesium is an environmentally friendly product. It is non-toxic and easy to recycle. In recent years the automobile industry has used an increasing quantity of magnesium. Lighter cars will reduce the consumption of petrol and thereby reduce carbon dioxide emissions. The illustration shows Norwegian cyclist, Dag Erik Pedersen, testing a bicycle with a magnesium frame.

Agriculture

In 1989 Norsk Hydro produced 11 million tons of artificial fertilizer. This helped to increase world food production and covered the food requirements of 200 million people. The company is investing large sums in research to discover how artificial fertilizers affect the natural ecological systems.
In 1990 Norsk Hydro was the largest producer of artificial fertilizer in the world, exporting to all continents.
In Asia artificial fertilizer is used to increase the rice harvest.

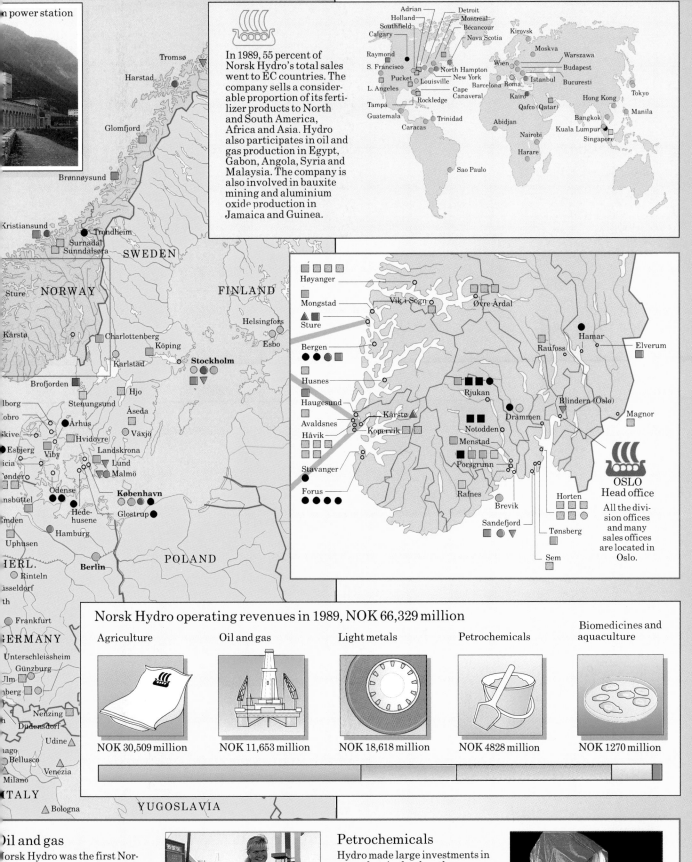

...n power station

Tromsø
Harstad

Glomfjord

Brønnøysund

Kristiansund
Surnadal
Sunndalsøra
Trondheim

SWEDEN

Sture
NORWAY
FINLAND

Kårstø
Charlottenberg
Helsingfors
Köping
Esbo
Karlstad
Stockholm

Brofjorden
Hjo
Åseda

...lborg
Stenungsund
Växjö
...obro
Århus
...kive
Hvidovre
Landskrona
...Esbjerg
Viby
Lund
...icia
Malmö
...ønder
Odense
København
...nsbüttel
Hede-
husene
Glostrup
...mden
Hamburg

Uphusen

POLAND

...IERL.
Rinteln
Berlin
...isseldorf
...th

Frankfurt

...ERMANY

Unterschleissheim
Günzburg
...lm
...nberg

Nenzing
Düdensdorf
...nago
Udine
Bellusco
Venezia
...Milano

ITALY
Bologna

YUGOSLAVIA

In 1989, 55 percent of Norsk Hydro's total sales went to EC countries. The company sells a considerable proportion of its fertilizer products to North and South America, Africa and Asia. Hydro also participates in oil and gas production in Egypt, Gabon, Angola, Syria and Malaysia. The company is also involved in bauxite mining and aluminium oxide production in Jamaica and Guinea.

Adrian
Holland
Southfield
Detroit
Montreal
Calgary
Bécancour
Nova Scotia
Kirovsk
Raymond
Moskva
S. Francisco
North Hampton
Warszawa
Pucket
Wien
Budapest
L. Angeles
Louisville
New York
Istanbul
Roma
Bucuresti
Barcelona
Cape
Tampa
Rockledge
Canaveral
Kairo
Hong Kong
Tokyo
Guatemala
Qafco (Qatar)
Bangkok
Manila
Trinidad
Caracas
Abidjan
Kuala Lumpur
Nairobi
Singapore
Harare
Sao Paulo

Høyanger
Mongstad
Vik i Sogn
Øvre Ardal
Sture
Bergen
Hamar
Raufoss
Elverum
Husnes
Haugesund
Rjukan
Blindern (Oslo)
Magnor
Avaldsnes
Kårstø
Kopervik
Notodden
Drammen
Håvik
Menstad
Stavanger
Porsgrunn
OSLO
Head office
Forus
Rafnes
Horten
Brevik
All the division offices and many sales offices are located in Oslo.
Sandefjord
Tønsberg
Sem

Norsk Hydro operating revenues in 1989, NOK 66,329 million

Agriculture	Oil and gas	Light metals	Petrochemicals	Biomedicines and aquaculture
NOK 30,509 million	NOK 11,653 million	NOK 18,618 million	NOK 4828 million	NOK 1270 million

Oil and gas

...orsk Hydro was the first Norwegian company to take part in ...il and gas exploration in the ...orth Sea. Today Hydro has ...ares in several oil and gas ...elds. Hydro was the first company in the world to use a specially ...quipped rig for exploratory drilling in the Arctic regions. Hydro ...as established a centre for oil ...esearch in Bergen. The company ...efines oil in its own refineries. ...etrol is sold from Norsk Hydro's ...etrol stations in Norway, ...weden and Denmark.

Petrochemicals

Hydro made large investments in petrochemicals when the company became involved in oil activities in the North Sea in the 1970s. A lot has been done to reduce environmental damage from the use of chlorine and mercury, but there is still a long way to go. Hydro is also working on recycling PVC waste for use in new products, e.g. pipes and floor coverings. Today it is difficult to imagine everyday life without plastic.

...NISIA
Malta

0   200 km

Kreta

Norway during the First World War

Norway was neutral after 1905. The Storting and the government wished to keep the country out of international conflicts. However, when the First World War broke out in the summer of 1914, Norway was in a delicate situation. In spite of the country's neutrality, the majority sympathised with the British, and the Norwegian economy was dependent on a good relationship with Britain. Britain provided essential goods, such as oil and coal, and the merchant fleet had to avoid a British blockade at any price. The British took advantage of this. In 1915 they forced Norway to stop most of its fish exports to Germany. Norway was spoken of as «the neutral ally».

This policy caused a tense relationship with Germany, and German submarines did a great deal of damage to the Norwegian merchant fleet. Half the fleet was sunk and over 2000 sailors lost their lives. The merchant fleet provided valuable support for Britain and her allies. Norwegian merchant vessels often sailed in the most dangerous waters.

The first two years of the war were highly lucrative for some Norwegians. Since there was a demand for Norwegian goods and services, the stock market boomed. This was particularly marked in the case of shipping stocks, but industrial stocks also showed a strong increase and some people made enormous profits from speculating on the market. However, most of the newly-rich later lost their fortunes.

Most people experienced increasing difficulties in the last two years of the war and teachers wrote reports of children who were tired and had headaches because they had too little food. The authorities tried to soften the effects of the hard times but the measures they introduced came rather late. All the municipalities established supply committees so that the State could control food supplies. A sugar monopoly and a corn monopoly were introduced and a number of products were rationed, including corn, flour, sugar, bread, coffee and tea. Rents were also controlled because they had risen sharply. The State Price Directorate, which was established in 1917 to implement government price policies, still exists today under a new name. The State intervened to control the everyday life of the people in a manner that was hitherto unknown.

The shortages and the way in which the newly-rich flaunted their wealth caused dissatisfaction among ordinary citizens and the war years intensified class differences in Norway.

Finance, Business and Industry between the Wars

After a short period of expansion from 1918 to 1920, Norway suffered from a long economic crisis which lasted right up to the outbreak of war in 1939. Unemployment among trade union members was over 15 per cent throughout most of this period. Both prices and the value of money showed strong fluctuations. This led to wage disagreements. The workers went on strike and the employers answered with lockouts.

The Bank of Norway's fiscal policy in the 1920s intensified the problem. Since the Bank had printed too many banknotes during the war, there was strong inflation

This drawing, from «Korsaren» magazine, shows Norway under pressure from the Great Powers during the First World War.

and a fall in the value of the krone when peace arrived. The Bank of Norway therefore introduced measures to strengthen the krone in relation to the pound and the gold standard. The Bank reduced the money supply and increased interest rates. In 1928 the value of the krone had reached the level which the central bank found desirable.

But the high rate of exchange created new problems. Since it was more difficult to raise loans and repay debts, industrial investments declined. People who already had loans also got into difficulties. They had to pay interest and instalments with kroner which were much more expensive than when the terms of the loans had been agreed.

Many farmers had mortgaged their farms in order to modernise their operations. A farmer who in 1924 had borrowed a sum which could be repaid by selling 10,000 litres of milk, had to sell 17,000 litres to cover the same loan two years later. Thousands of farmers were unable to cope with the increased debt burden. They were forced to sell their farms and find work in competition with other unemployed people.

Edvard Munch (1863–1944) is the best known Norwegian artist abroad. In the period between the two World Wars he was influenced by the advance of the working class. This painting is called «Workers in Snow». In a letter of 1929, Munch wrote: «Now is the age of the workers. Perhaps art will once again belong to everyone.»

Forced sale at Skulle-rud Farm, Oslo, in September 1934. The police are there to pre-vent disturbances.

Most of the bankrupt farmers did not lose their farms, however, because the local community often agreed to boycott the forced sales. They also threatened any prospective buyers likely to bid for the properties. When there were no buyers, the banks usually reduced the debt and let the old owner take over the farm again.

Many farmers tried to solve their difficulties by increasing production. Since people in the towns had less money to buy food with, there was a surplus of agricultural produce. Competition between the farmers increased and prices fell. Something had to be done.

In cooperation with the government, the farmers established sales cooperatives. These cooperatives were empowered to control the turnover of agricultural produce. For example, the milk cooperatives decided how much milk should go for consumption and how much should be used for the production of cheese and butter. Cooperatives determined prices, organised exports and were allowed to introduce tariffs on the produce. These funds were used to stabilise prices. This type of regulation of the market became a pattern for agriculture in many other countries.

Fishermen were particularly hard hit by the inter-war crisis. They had also borrowed money for new equipment in the post-1905 boom. When export prices dropped and loans became more expensive in the 1920s, many fishermen's families experienced real poverty. About half of all adult males in the northernmost counties had fishing as their main or subsidiary source of income. Many of them could no longer afford to own decked boats with engines and large nets. Instead they had to fish with hand-held lines from open boats. Incomes fell drastically and in many coastal municipalities both adults and children suffered from undernourishment and an unbalanced diet.

The world economic crisis, which began in the USA in 1929, reached Norway the following year. On an average, one third of the work force was unemployed between 1931 and 1933. Taking the 1930s as a whole, up to one quarter of the population was dependent on poor relief. In 1931 over 7.5 million working days were lost due to industrial disputes.

Unemployment in the 1930s was not only due to the economic crisis. The numbers of young people reaching working age at that time were larger than before and the USA

had shut its doors to mass immigration. At the same time, more women were marrying later and many of them were seeking employment.

With falling prices and increasing wage costs and interest rates, many companies went out of business. The banks lost large sums on bad debts. People were afraid of losing their savings and rushed to the banks to withdraw their money. The State provided considerable support for the banks, but this did not do much to alleviate the problem. Many banks went out of business and their depositors' money was lost.

The mid-war years were not only a time of crisis. Statistics show that the gross national product doubled and industrial production increased by approximately 80 per cent. All the same, there were no more industrial jobs in 1939 than there had been in 1915. One of the main reasons for this was that companies introduced new machinery and rationalised production methods on the American pattern.

Those who were lucky enough to keep their jobs got more for their money than

before. They bought electric cookers, irons and water heaters and installed new furniture, lavatories and bathrooms in their homes. Many people could also afford to buy radios and the most well-to-do bought cars. With their new spare time, people used more money on sporting equipment, such as skis, skates and bicycles. Going to the cinema, reading magazines, smoking cigarettes and eating chocolate were no longer luxuries.

Most of the consumer goods that came onto the market in the inter-war years were produced by newly-established, small companies. Norway, like so many other countries, increased import duties in order to protect domestic industry. These policies affected the export industry, however. From 1930 to 1939 the export share of industrial production dropped from 57 to 42 per cent.

Although many ships had to be laid up in the worst years of the crisis, the inter-war period was a time of growth for the shipping industry. In the 1930s only Great Britain and the USA had bigger merchant fleets. Norwegian shipowners were among

The Café of the Unemployed was run by the trade union movement in Oslo from 1929 to 1939. The unemployed were given one free meal a day.

In the period between the wars the tobacco industry tried to persuade women to start smoking. Norway was the first country in the western world to prohibit tobacco advertising, in 1975.

The poster on the right shows how town and country were linked by radio waves.

the first to replace steamships with motor vessels. In 1939 Norway had the most modern merchant fleet in the world, including many specialised vessels, such as tankers and cold-storage ships. At the same time, many shipowners transferred their interests from the tramp trade to shipping lines with fixed routes across the oceans of the world. It also became more usual to sign long-term freight contracts, the oil companies being the most important customers. Norwegian shipowners no longer attracted customers by offering low rates on old ships with crews on starvation wages. They now won new market shares under the motto «speed and service».

The shipowners ordered most of their new ships from British and Swedish shipyards and most of the capital was borrowed abroad. At the end of the 1930s shipping played a key role in the export economy. Freight income accounted for about 40 per cent of the country's foreign earnings.

Ever since Svend Foyn invented the harpoon gun in the 1860s, Norwegians had played a major role in the whaling industry. Up to the beginning of the 1900s, the whaling grounds were mainly along the

Norwegian coast and in the North Atlantic. When the whale stocks in the north showed signs of depletion, there was a search for new hunting grounds and the Antarctic became the most important whaling area. Processing plants for the blue whale were established on several British islands in the Antarctic, South Georgia being the most important of these.

The profitability of the whaling industry was greatly increased when the fat industry introduced a new hardening process, making it possible to use whale oil in margarine production. However, the Norwegian whalers were in danger of being excluded from this growing market. The British raised duties on Norwegian catches and prohibited the building of new factories on land. This forced the Norwegians to build large, floating factory ships, where they processed the blue whale on the open sea outside British territorial waters. The hauling slips on the factory ships were an especially important invention. They made it possible to haul the carcasses up on deck, where they were cut up and boiled in large vats.

The boom did not last for long. The price

A whale being hauled onto a factory ship in the 1930s.

of whale oil sank drastically during the 1930s and the world economic crisis led to a fall in demand. At the same time whaling capacity increased, particularly due to the participation of the Japanese and German whaling fleets. The Norwegian share of world whale oil production therefore declined from 65 to 30 percent between 1927 and 1938.

Fishing, Whaling and Sealing

Sealing ships off Greenland. International opposition to seal hunting grew in the 1980s, leading to a crisis in a traditional industry.

Exports of clipfish (dried cod) became increasingly important from the mid-eighteenth century onwards. The herring fisheries provided a good livelihood for the coastal population, but the herring stocks disappeared at certain periods. Cod never disappeared completely, but catches varied consideraby from one season to the next. Great progress was made in the fishing industry around 1900. Fishing boats were built with decks and engines, so the fishermen were able to go out to the fishing banks. New equipment, such as drift nets and purse seine nets, led to increasingly large catches. After the Second World War the catches were even bigger, as the fishing boats had trawl gallows and ring nets while sonar and echo-sounders made it easier to find the fish. Factories were built on land for the production of frozen fish, fish fillets, fishmeal and fish oil.

Coastal whaling has long traditions in Norway and has no connection with the pelagic whaling carried out by Vestfold shipowners. Seal hunting began round Svalbard in the 1790s and later spread to the Barents Sea, Greenland and Newfoundland.

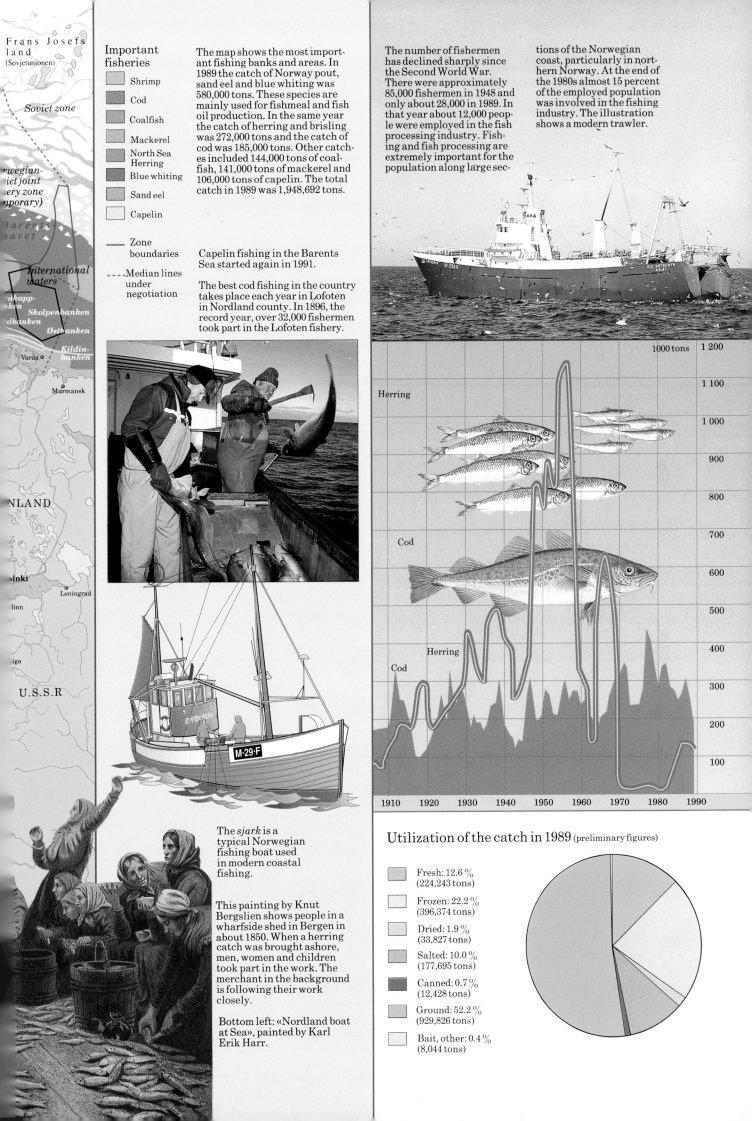

Frans Josefs
land
(Sovjetunionen)

Soviet zone

rwegian-
iet joint
ery zone
porary)

Bare
avet

International
waters

kapp-
ken
Skolpenbanken
dbanken
Østbanken
Kildin-
banken
Vardø

Murmansk

NLAND

sinki

Leningrad

linn

iga

U.S.S.R

Important fisheries

- Shrimp
- Cod
- Coalfish
- Mackerel
- North Sea Herring
- Blue whiting
- Sand eel
- Capelin

—— Zone boundaries

----- Median lines under negotiation

The map shows the most important fishing banks and areas. In
1989 the catch of Norway pout,
sand eel and blue whiting was
580,000 tons. These species are
mainly used for fishmeal and fish
oil production. In the same year
the catch of herring and brisling
was 272,000 tons and the catch of
cod was 185,000 tons. Other catches included 144,000 tons of coalfish, 141,000 tons of mackerel and
106,000 tons of capelin. The total
catch in 1989 was 1,948,692 tons.

Capelin fishing in the Barents
Sea started again in 1991.

The best cod fishing in the country
takes place each year in Lofoten
in Nordland county. In 1896, the
record year, over 32,000 fishermen
took part in the Lofoten fishery.

The *sjark* is a
typical Norwegian
fishing boat used
in modern coastal
fishing.

This painting by Knut
Bergslien shows people in a
wharfside shed in Bergen in
about 1850. When a herring
catch was brought ashore,
men, women and children
took part in the work. The
merchant in the background
is following their work
closely.

Bottom left: «Nordland boat
at Sea», painted by Karl
Erik Harr.

The number of fishermen
has declined sharply since
the Second World War.
There were approximately
85,000 fishermen in 1948 and
only about 28,000 in 1989. In
that year about 12,000 people were employed in the fish
processing industry. Fishing and fish processing are
extremely important for the
population along large sections of the Norwegian
coast, particularly in northern Norway. At the end of
the 1980s almost 15 percent
of the employed population
was involved in the fishing
industry. The illustration
shows a modern trawler.

Utilization of the catch in 1989 (preliminary figures)

- Fresh: 12.6 % (224,243 tons)
- Frozen: 22.2 % (396,374 tons)
- Dried: 1.9 % (33,827 tons)
- Salted: 10.0 % (177,695 tons)
- Canned: 0.7 % (12,428 tons)
- Ground: 52.2 % (929,826 tons)
- Bait, other: 0.4 % (8,044 tons)

Non-socialist Coalition Policies between the Wars

The non-socialist parties won a majority at all the elections between the wars but were unable to establish a stable government. Norway had nine different governments from 1918 to 1935, which were in power for an average of only one-and-a-half years each. Nearly all of them were minority governments and most were led by the Liberal Party.

Although the labour movement grew stronger and some sections of it spoke of revolution and the class struggle, the Liberals would not join a broad, anti-socialist, conservative block. The party wanted to rise above class differences and utilise the resources of the state to help the weaker members of society. The Liberals believed that social reforms, price controls and laws limiting the power of the capitalists would remove much of the basis for disaffection in the working classes.

The Liberals were strongest in the south and west of the country, where people were supporters of the New Norwegian language, the temperance movement and the Christian lay movements. The party also wanted to reduce duties on agricultural products so that food prices would be lower. This led to conflict with the farmers, who founded their own party, the Farmers' Party, in 1920 and took over many of the Liberal supporters. The party obtained between 11.6 and 15.9 of the vote at every election up to 1936.

The Farmers' Party believed that the Liberals were too tolerant of the labour movement, too supportive of government intervention in business and industry and too little concerned with limiting government and municipal expenditure. In the 1920s the party opposed allocations for relief work for the unemployed. They wanted the government to support agriculture by subsidising the clearing of new land and corn production, so that the country would be as self-supporting as possible and conditions for the farmers would be improved. The party was convinced that a strong farming community was the best defence against the revolutionary socialists.

In the 1920s and 1930s the Conservative Party emerged more clearly as the party of business and industry and had a firm foothold among the non-socialist middle classes in the towns, particularly in the southeast. The Conservatives were those who were most concerned at the increase in government responsibilities and expenditure. They maintained that taxes and public expenditure should be reduced as much as possible in times of crisis so that business and industry would be encouraged to invest in new enterprises. The Conservatives were also supported by voters who were afraid of the socialists. The party emphasised «law and order» and promised to react strongly if revolutionary elements made good their threats against middle-class society. The Conservative Party was sceptical about the New Norwegian language and had liberal views in matters concerning religion and morality.

Disagreement on alcohol policies particularly affected cooperation between the Conservative and Liberal parties in the 1920s. It also led to internal conflicts in most of the other parties. During the war, the Liberal government had introduced a temporary ban on sales of spirits because most of the corn and potato harvests had to be used for food. This decision was supported by the temperance movement, which had grown in strength since the early 1800s. Since then alcoholism had become a serious problem, particularly affecting the weakest in society.

After the war, the temperance movement wanted to make prohibition permanent and to extend it to cover fortified wines. In a referendum in 1919 there was a majority for these proposals and soon afterwards the Storting passed a law forbidding the sale of beverages with an alcohol content of over 12 percent.

The new arrangement had several unfortunate effects, however. There was widespread smuggling, home-distilling and illegal trading in spirits. But growing

criminality was not the greatest threat to prohibition. France, Spain and Portugal issued sharp protests because they lost old export markets for wines and spirits. Spain and Portugal replied by increasing customs duties on Norwegian fish. Successive governments negotiated agreements with the wine-growing countries, who imposed hard conditions for the removal of trade barriers: Norway would have to consent to import large quantities of wines and spirits for warehousing. These agreements were rejected by the Storting and three governments had to resign because the majority did not approve their alcohol policies.

In 1923 the problems for fish exporters were so great that the Storting decided to remove the ban on fortified wines. A new referendum three years later showed that a majority of the population also wanted to remove the ban on spirits. The Storting complied with this recommendation but at the same time ensured that the state would have a considerable influence on alcohol sales. A new company, *A/S Vinmonopolet,* was established as a state monopoly for the sale of wines and spirits. This arrangement is still in force today.

As a result of widespread strikes and revolutionary threats from the labour movement, the Storting passed several laws to protect non-socialist society. Prison sentences were introduced for people who prevented strike-breakers from working. The same punishment awaited those who supported illegal strikes, refused to do military service or agitated against the military establishment. Several Labour Party leaders were jailed for offences against these laws.

The non-socialist governments also sent in police and soldiers to protect blacklegs. Important employers' organisations, such as the Bank Association, the Federation of Norwegian Industries and the Norwegian Farmers' Union, cooperated in building up «Norwegian Community Aid», which supplied new labour to industry during labour disputes. There was also a secret

The sharp class distinctions between the wars were also seen in the art of the period. In this painting, Erik Werenskiold has shown the mixed feelings of the bourgeoisie when they were confronted with the problems of the poor.

stand-by force in the army, composed of «reliable» troops. In addition, the political authorities agreed to establish a civil defence force which received military training from army officers. This «Community Defence Force» had about 10,000 members.

Norway also developed its own branch of the European Fascist movement. *Nasjonal Samling,* (National Unification) the Norwegian version of the National Socialist Party, was founded in 1933 and led by Vidkun Quisling. The party was inspired by Mussolini's Italy, German Nazism and the Finnish Lappo movement. It appealed to people who were dissatisfied with non-socialist democracy and wanted to oppose the labour movement, and gained from the frustration which had developed during the worst years of crisis. In many rural municipalities NS was supported by farmers and foresters who felt that the stability of the old farming communities was being threatened by outside forces. They believed that the crisis in the rural economy was due to the problems of industrial society and that the labour movement, with its foreign connections, was causing unnecessary conflicts in rural areas.

NS wanted to stop the class struggle and unite the whole people under one party and one leader. The Nordic race was regarded as superior to all others and people were told to fight against Jews, Bolsheviks and other «inferior» foreigners. NS glorified the history of the Norwegian Middle Ages. The party symbol was the old Germanic sun cross.

NS polled only a few percent of the votes at elections during the 1930s and had no representatives in the Storting. There were also internal disagreements, and many members left the party. By 1939 NS had been reduced to a small, isolated sect. Nobody expected the party to be given its historic opportunity in the following year with the help of German bayonets.

Division and Unification in the Labour Movement

In 1919 the Labour Party abandoned the social-democratic course which the party had followed since its foundation in 1887. A revolutionary wing had taken over control of the party towards the end of the First World War. It had lost much of its faith in being able to improve conditions for the working class under the old regime. Negotiations with employers and participation in parliamentary activity were no longer enough. A resolution of March 1918 stated that the party had become a «revolutionary party of class struggle» with the right to use «revolutionary mass action in the fight for the economic liberation of the working classes».

The radicalisation of the labour movement must be seen in the light of the fact that living conditions for large sections of the population had deteriorated. In 1917 prices increased sharply and lack of goods, black-marketeering and speculation were everyday phenomena. Newly-rich stock-market speculators lived in luxury, while many people had to struggle to make ends meet. In the autumn, news came from Russia that the Bolsheviks had overthrown the rule of the Czar and established a new workers' state. Workers' and soldiers' councils on the pattern of the Russian soviets were set up in many places, and in spring 1918 the revolutionary wing won a majority at the Labour Party Conference. The Norwegian Labour Party was the only European social-democratic party to choose to join the Communist International, Comintern, which was based in Moscow. This led to a party split. In 1921 the right wing broke away and founded a new social democratic party.

It was not long before conflicts arose between the Labour Party and Comintern. There was growing concern in Norway over the Soviet Communists' demands for all member parties to follow blindly orders from Moscow. In 1923 a majority of the Labour Party passed a resolution to break with the Communist International. The minority founded the Norwegian Communist Party (NKP), which was received as a new member of Comintern. During the late 1920s NKP lost members and voters to the Labour Party and in the 1930s the

Banner of the Rjukan workers' union, expressing the revolutionary fervour that characterised the labour movement in the 1920s.

Communists did not manage to win a single seat in the Storting.

Both before and after leaving Comintern there were signs indicating that the revolutionary fervour of the Labour Party was in decline. In 1921 the Norwegian Federation of Trade Unions brought about 150,000 men out on strike because employers wanted to reduce seamen's wages by one third. The strike was a fiasco. The trade union movement did not have the economic backing to support the striking workers in a long-drawn-out dispute. After only two weeks the strike was called off and the workers had to accept a 17 per cent reduction in wages.

The bitter conflict between the Labour party, the social democrats and NKP exhausted the strength of the labour movement and membership of the Trade Union Federation declined. It is therefore not surprising that it was the trade union movement which exerted pressure to end the party split, and their efforts were rewarded. In 1927 the Labour Party and the Social Democrats joined forces and stood for election on a programme emphasising the old social-democratic values. The party now intended to win a majority with the help of peaceful reforms passed by elected institutions. The election was a success. The Labour Party became the largest party in the country and has been so ever since.

The non-socialist parties still had a majority in the Storting but negotiations among them led to deadlock. Everyone was surprised when King Håkon intervened and gave the task of forming a government to the republican Labour Party, which every year voted against the allocation of funds to the royal family.

The country's first Labour government took over in January 1928. It presented an extremely provocative programme, promising to «prepare the changeover to a socialist society». Industrialists and bankers immediately transferred large sums of money abroad and the government was defeated after only two weeks. The non-socialist parties quickly agreed on a new government when the economic stability of the country was threatened.

These events led to a strengthening of the positions of the radical elements in the Labour Party. At the 1930 party conference the party adopted a programme which included much of the old revolutionary language. It caused concern among the non-socialists, who started a strong counter-offensive prior to the 1930 general election. This ended in defeat for the Labour Party.

The disastrous election results contributed to a loss of support for the revolutionary wing of the Labour Party. But unemployment and the social crisis also helped to steer the party onto a more moderate course. Increasing numbers of people demanded that the party should formulate a new policy which would put the country back on its feet. In 1933 the Labour Party launched a crisis programme which promised full employment. Many of the proposals were based on the ideas of the British economist, John Maynard Keynes, and the experiences of the Soviet planned economy. The programme broke with the principle that the state should save money in times of depression. It was now suggested that the state should take up large loans to finance programmes to reduce unemployment. In a «Norwegian three-year plan» in autumn 1933, the Labour Party proposed that the state should invest large sums in new agriculture, industrial development, power stations, roads and railways. The means of production should not be nationalised, but the state should be given greater powers to regulate and control the economy.

This new policy was the main reason for resounding support for Labour at the 1933 general election. The growth of fascism in Europe made the party more positive towards non-socialist democracy, and in 1935 the Norwegian Employers' Confederation negotiated a basic agreement for employees. This agreement laid down rules for wage negotiations and collective agreements and ensured the right of workers to form trade unions and elect spokesmen.

Fresco in Oslo City Hall, painted by Reidar Aulie (1904–1977), showing workers demonstrating for their rights.

After the 1933 election there was growing unrest in the Farmers' Party due to forced sales and unemployment in rural areas. The party presented several proposals for greater allocations for agriculture but the Liberal government rejected them. This led to closer ties between the Farmers' Party and the Labour Party. In 1935 they reached a compromise: the Labour Party formed a government and promised to increase allocations to the rural economy.

Under Prime Minister Johan Nygaardsvold, the Labour Party remained in power until 1945. In the pre-war years it followed moderate reform policies, and the Labour Party became an accepted participant in parliamentary democracy. The labour movement was now more concerned with increasing production and social welfare than with the class struggle. The government created optimism and an atmosphere of cooperation in politics and economic life. It also reaped the benefits of an im-provement in the international economy, which led to greater demand for Norwegian goods.

The non-socialist majority in the Storting rejected the proposal of taking up large state loans and presenting deficit budgets to stimulate the economy. However, the Labour Party had the support of the Farmers' Party and the Liberals to increase taxation and duties. More money could therefore be used to provide employment and implement social reforms. The government passed a new law protecting the rights of workers, which ensured that all employees would have an 8-hour day and nine days' holiday a year. The health insurance scheme was extended to cover new groups of employees, and old-age pensions and unemployment benefits were introduced. These reforms enlarged the scope of government responsibilities.

Outdoor Life

«I am done with the lowland life. Up here on the heights are freedom, God, Men do but grope in the valley.» (Henrik Ibsen, *On the Heights*, 1859)

Many of the outdoor leisure activities in Norway today are rooted in the everyday life of country people. Early in the 19th century, well-to-do town dwellers discovered the joys of the open air and the recreational opportunities offered by the countryside. The trend was set by British anglers, huntsmen, mountaineers and hikers who came to Norway.

In 1868 the Norwegian Mountain Touring Association (DNT) was founded. For 100 years the association has built cabins providing overnight accommodation and marked and signposted paths and tracks.

Nowadays outdoor life is an important part of the Norwegian life style. Many Norwegians walk – or ski – in the forests on Sundays and many spend weekends and holidays at cabins in the mountains or by the sea.

Gjendebu in the Jotunheimen Mountains was the first of DNT's cabins. It opened in 1871.

The writer Aasmund Olavsson Vinje (1818–1870) was one of the founders of DNT. In the columns of his newspaper he encouraged people in the towns to go to the mountains.

Polar explorer and scientist Fridtjof Nansen (1861–1930) and his wife Eva (1858–1907) on skis. The couple became the ideal of young people who wanted to lead an outdoor life. Eva Nansen was the first well-known townswoman to ski in the mountains. She had a special skiing outfit, designed by her husband.

Therese Bertheau (1861–1936) was the first woman mountaineer in Norway. She is photographed here before a climb in Sogn at the turn of the century.

In the 1820s the first anglers came to Norway from Great Britain. This illustration shows fly fishing at Tana in Finnmark county. It was customary in northern Norway for Sami to help foreigners with their fishing.

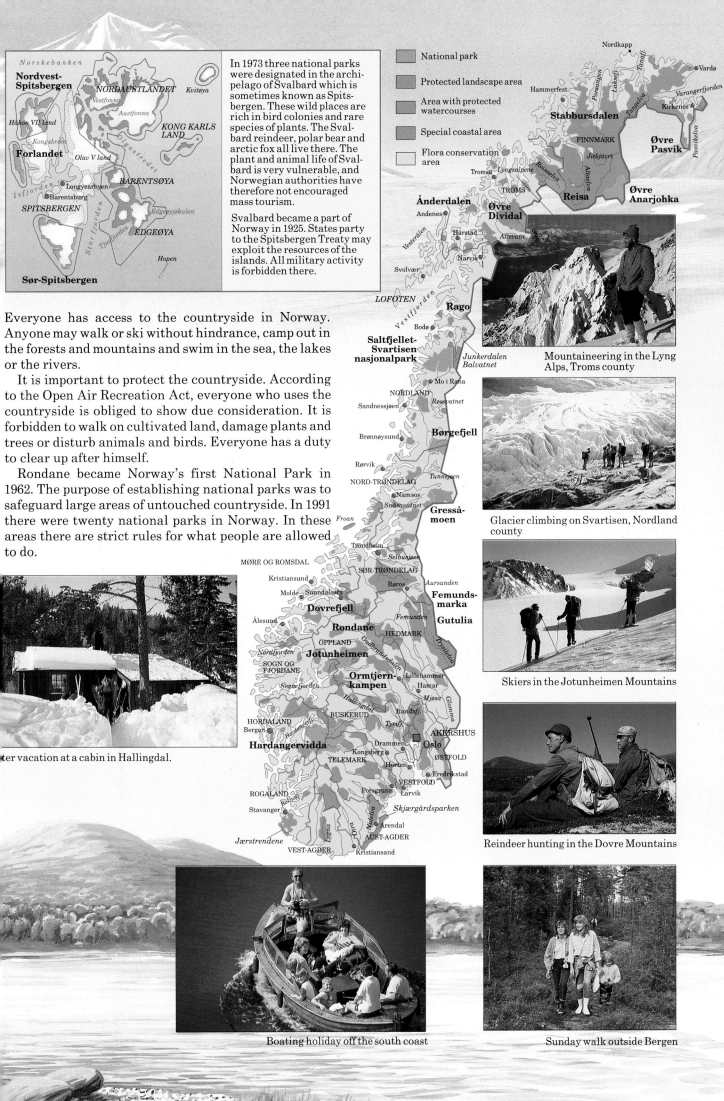

In 1973 three national parks were designated in the archipelago of Svalbard which is sometimes known as Spitsbergen. These wild places are rich in bird colonies and rare species of plants. The Svalbard reindeer, polar bear and arctic fox all live there. The plant and animal life of Svalbard is very vulnerable, and Norwegian authorities have therefore not encouraged mass tourism.

Svalbard became a part of Norway in 1925. States party to the Spitsbergen Treaty may exploit the resources of the islands. All military activity is forbidden there.

National park

Protected landscape area

Area with protected watercourses

Special coastal area

Flora conservation area

Everyone has access to the countryside in Norway. Anyone may walk or ski without hindrance, camp out in the forests and mountains and swim in the sea, the lakes or the rivers.

It is important to protect the countryside. According to the Open Air Recreation Act, everyone who uses the countryside is obliged to show due consideration. It is forbidden to walk on cultivated land, damage plants and trees or disturb animals and birds. Everyone has a duty to clear up after himself.

Rondane became Norway's first National Park in 1962. The purpose of establishing national parks was to safeguard large areas of untouched countryside. In 1991 there were twenty national parks in Norway. In these areas there are strict rules for what people are allowed to do.

ter vacation at a cabin in Hallingdal.

Mountaineering in the Lyng Alps, Troms county

Glacier climbing on Svartisen, Nordland county

Skiers in the Jotunheimen Mountains

Reindeer hunting in the Dovre Mountains

Boating holiday off the south coast

Sunday walk outside Bergen

Foreign and Defence Policy

At the end of the First World War the victorious powers agreed to found a world organisation to safeguard peace. Under the League of Nations Charter, member states were obliged to intervene by imposing sanctions against any country that started a war. When Norway decided to join, it followed that the country might be forced to choose sides in the event of conflicts between the Great Powers. This was an important reason why many politicians were reluctant to drop the principle of neutrality. When the question of membership was debated in the Storting, however, a large majority supported the new peace organisation. The chances of war seemed slight and many were concerned to be on a good footing with the western powers upon which Norway was so dependent, both politically and economically. It was not easy to break away from «polite society», especially once Great Britain had joined.

Norway was involved in the humanitarian work of the League of Nations at the beginning of the 1920s. Fridtjof Nansen made an important contribution in Russia, Greece and Turkey as High Commissioner for Refugees and led the emergency effort during the famine in the Ukraine in 1921. In the following year he was rewarded with the Nobel Peace Prize.

Norway took active part in the work on disarmament and wished to set an example in international cooperation. To this end, Norway established arbitration agreements with the other Scandinavian countries and a number of other states. The signatories agreed to solve conflicts by means of negotiation, mediation and arbitration. However, since most of the Great Powers declined to sign, the agreements were of little value.

When the international situation deteriorated in the latter half of the 1930s, Norway and the other Scandinavian countries announced that they no longer felt obliged to participate in League of Nations sanctions. After this, Norway relied on the old policy of neutrality.

During the peace negotiations after the First World War, Norway claimed sovereignty over Svalbard. A treaty was signed to this effect, but all the signatory countries were entitled to engage in commercial activities there. At the end of the 1920s, Norway also gained Jan Mayen, Bouvet Island and Peter I Island. The two latter islands were of particular interest in connection with whaling in the Antarctic. Norway also claimed large areas on the Antarctic mainland, and in 1939 Queen Maud's Land came under Norwegian sovereignty.

In the 1920s a conflict arose between sealers from western Norway and the Danish authorities in connection with sealing and fishing rights in East Greenland. A nationalistic movement of «Greenland Societies» grew up in several areas of the country, agitating for Norway to annexe the disputed area. The movement was delighted when a few activists occupied East Greenland and were supported by the government. In accordance with the arbitration agreement between Denmark and Norway, the conflict was brought before the International Court of Justice in the Hague, which awarded full sovereignty over all Greenland to Denmark.

Optimism about the prospects for peace in the 1920s naturally led to cuts in defence spending and in 1932 the Storting passed a new defence plan. A small watch-keeping force would be established, and if there was a danger of war, larger units would be mobilised. The Ministry of Foreign Affairs was empowered to notify the government when it judged the mobilisation of extra forces to be necessary.

In spite of increasing international tension in the following years, these forces were not built up as envisaged in the plan. There was a strong belief that Norway would be able to stay out of any new wars. Many people believed that the peaceful conclusion of the union conflict with Sweden was due to good diplomacy on the part of the Norwegians. Few people pointed out that increased defence efforts and

mobilisation prior to 1905 had strengthened the Norwegian negotiating position.
Most people were also convinced that it
was the government's wise foreign policy,
not military strength, which had prevented the country from becoming involved in
the First World War.

The likelihood of other countries wishing to invade Norway was regarded as
minimal. Great Britain was thought to be
the state most likely to want to control
Norwegian territory in times of crisis, but
this did not mean that the British had
enemy status. The general opinion was
that the British fleet would prevent attacks by other powers. If Norway were
forced to choose sides in a new war, most
people would support Great Britain.

The majority of politicians were
convinced that Norway would be unable to
repel an attack by any of the Great Powers,
however much the country prepared for
war. They argued that a strong defence
would seem provocative and did not wish
to risk material losses or human lives. The
economic crisis also made it difficult to
increase the defence budget. Nor were the
defence plans based on the assumption
that Norwegian forces would be involved
in a long war. Their purpose was to indica-
te that Norway would not condone occupation.

When the Labour Party came to power
in 1935, many people were afraid that they
would pursue their anti-militarist policies.
This did not happen, however. The party
followed the defence policy that had been
drawn up by the Liberals and supported
the main principles of the defence plan of
the early 1930s. In the years prior to 1940,
the Labour Party, the Liberals and the
Farmers' Party were agreed on defence
policy.

Great Power Rivalry over Norway

In September 1939 Germany carried out a
surprise attack on Poland and the Second
World War had begun.

The government stated that Norway
would maintain strict neutrality and estab-

*Fridtjof Nansen
(1861–1930) photo-
graphed during the
effort to help refugees in
the Soviet Union in the
early 1920s. Nansen is
standing in the door-
way of the train.*

Adolf Hitler and some of his senior officers visiting the Norwegian fjords in 1934.

lished a watch-keeping force on the 1914 pattern. The navy, air force and anti-aircraft units were called up. Only some of the coastal forts and a few army divisions were put on war alert. The Ministry of Foreign Affairs saw no reason for recommending the comprehensive mobilisation provided for in the defence plan. Most people thought the chances of a German attack were slight. Any British and French operations would be met with symbolic resistance. Thus there was no need for comprehensive mobilisation of the army.

After the outbreak of war, the French government proposed the initiation of military operations in Scandinavia. They wanted to involve Hitler in more distant countries to ease the pressure on France. A Franco-British campaign in the north would also meet the demands from the opposition in the French National Assembly for a more active defence strategy. In addition, the French were intent on stopping Swedish iron ore exports to the

German armaments industry. Most of the ore was shipped from Narvik in northern Norway.

With the exception of the First Lord of the Admiralty, Winston Churchill, the British government was at first uninterested in the French proposals. During the winter of 1939–40, however, the British also became more keen on action. They were increasingly uneasy about the way in which German ships were avoiding the British blockade in the North Sea by sailing through neutral waters along the Norwegian coast. London's dissatisfaction with Norwegian policy of neutrality increased sharply in December 1939, when three British merchant ships were torpedoed inside the Norwegian three-mile limit. After this the British made it clear to the Norwegian government that Royal Navy ships would operate in Norwegian waters. The Norwegians protested, to no avail. In February 1940 the British went into action. The destroyer «*Cossack*» attacked the

German merchant ship *«Altmark»*, which had sought refuge in the Jøssing Fjord near Egersund. The *«Altmark»* had about 300 British prisoners-of-war on board. Seven Germans lost their lives when the British boarded the ship and freed the prisoners. Two Norwegian coastguard ships which were in the fjord at the time did not intervene in the episode.

After the Soviet Union's attack on Finland in November 1939, the British and French began to plan military action in northern Scandinavia. They decided to land troops in Narvik which would move east to take control of the Kiruna mines and help the Finns in their Winter War. The western Allies expected Germany to attempt to prevent this. They therefore mobilised a large force which was to land in Trondheim, Bergen and Stavanger to secure support points against German counter-attacks. However, these operations were cancelled in mid-March 1940 when Finland signed a peace treaty with the Soviet Union.

In France this decision led to the fall of the Deladier government. The new government increased the pressure on the British to mount a campaign in Scandinavia. After hard negotiations they agreed to lay mines along the Norwegian coast on 8 April. The idea was that the minefields would force German ships out into international waters, where they could be attacked more easily. At the same time, an army force was set up in Great Britain to be sent to Norway if it became clear that the Germans intended to land on the Norwegian coast. The British believed that the chances of such a counter-attack were small.

In the first months of the war, the German admiralty tried in vain to convince Hitler that it was necessary to capture bases on the Norwegian coast. The navy feared that it would be locked into the Baltic. It wanted improved opportunities for attacking England and wished to secure control of the North Atlantic.

Only after the leader of NS, Vidkun Quisling, had visited Berlin in December

1939 did Hitler order his chiefs of staff to plan for a German occupation of Norway. In a conversation with Hitler, Quisling had proposed that Norwegians and Germans should join forces to fight against Jews and Communists. These arguments may have made an impression on Hitler, because they suited his ideological vision of creating a «Greater Germanic», Nazi Europe with a common front against the Communist Soviet Union.

The *«Altmark»* affair convinced Hitler that Norway was unable to defend her neutrality. Preparations for the invasion were intensified and at the beginning of March 1940 operations against Denmark and Norway had top priority. On 3 April 1940 the first ships of the invasion fleet sailed north from German harbours. The date of the invasion was to be 9 April.

The coffins of dead Germans from the «Altmark» being put ashore at the Jøssing Fjord.

WAR AND
OCCUPATION
1940–1945

The 1940 Campaign

During the course of 9 April the Germans succeeded in occupying the positions they intended along the Norwegian coast. Their attack came as a great surprise, and resistance was weak. Only at the Oscarsborg fortress not far from Oslo did the invaders encounter any problems. Shots fired from the fortress destroyed the heavy cruiser «Blücher». On board were several key figures and special troops who had been assigned the task of controlling the capital. The sinking of this ship gave the King, government and members of the Storting the opportunity to escape. They went in the first instance to the small town of Elverum. There the Storting authorised the government to take independent decisions until the country should once again be free.

Nevertheless the Germans had good reason to be satisfied with their attack on Norway from the military point of view. It was the first combined operation in military history in which army, navy and air force worked as a team, and troops and equipment were carried in transport aircraft and ships. Once again the German military machine showed its might. With superior fire power from automatic weapons, tanks, artillery and bombers, it crushed resistance.

Despite the overwhelming odds, the Norwegian government decided to put up a fight. It was forced to take sides, and chose the side of Great Britain. A negotiated settlement with the Germans became unthinkable when Vidkun Quisling proclaimed himself Prime Minister, and Hitler gave him his support. And so the government put its trust in the Allies who promised to send help.

After the middle of April British forces disembarked at Andalsnes and Namsos, but to little avail. They were too few, insufficiently trained, and poorly equipped. The fiasco of this expedition led to the fall of the government in Britain. Winston Churchill replaced Neville Chamberlain as Prime Minister.

In just three weeks the Germans had won control of southern Norway, but fighting continued around Narvik in the north. British, French, Polish and Norwegian troops managed to drive the Germans out of the town and isolated them in a mountainous area near the Swedish border. This was the first successful military operation carried out by Allied forces in the Second

Opposite page: German troops during the fighting in Valdres. The Germans suffered about 5300 casualties (killed, wounded and missing in action) in the attack on Norway. Total Allied casualties were about 4900, the majority British.

World War. Nevertheless, even though at the beginning of June the German divisions were on the brink of defeat, the Allied supreme command decided to abandon the siege. Hitler's attack on France and the Benelux countries made it necessary to transfer all troops to continental Europe.

On 7 June 1940 the royal family and the government left for Britain in order to continue the fight from there. It was to be five years before they could return to a free Norway.

Norwegian soldiers during the April 1940 campaign. 860 Norwegian soldiers and over 300 civilians were killed.

German Policy for Occupied Norway

When the Germans launched their attack on Norway, their idea was to reach an accommodation with the government and establish an administration of occupation

NORGE 4·00

HEIM · ÆTT FEDRELAND

NASJONAL SAMLINGS KVINNEORGANISASJON

Hjelpen fra England

MOT BOLSJEVISMEN

MED WAFFEN-SS OG DEN NORSKE LEGION MOT DEN FELLES FIENDE...

ALT FOR NORGE

Posters showing important features of Nazi propaganda. The Norwegian National Socialist Party wanted women to join a new women's movement. NS also warned against the consequences of the royal family and the government cooperating with the British, and ran an intense campaign to enlist Norwegian youth in the war against the Soviet Union.

as they did in Denmark. This plan they had to give up, because they failed to capture the government and the royal family. In the confusion of 9 April, Quisling improvised a coup and formed a government which was recognised by Hitler. The result of this was more determined opposition, and only a week later the Quisling government was replaced by the Administrative Council with responsibility for civilian rule in the occupied areas. The members of this council were appointed by the Supreme Court from government departments and the major trade and employers' associations.

At the same time, Hitler set up a Reich Commissariat headed by Josef Terboven, and this was the centre of power throughout the German occupation. Terboven embarked on negotiations with members of the Administrative Council, the Supreme Court, the major organisations and the presidium of the Storting. His goal was the replacement of the Nygaardsvold government by a «Council of the Realm» which would be approved by the Storting. Many people thought that Germany was on the verge of winning the war, and the Norwegian negotiators went to great lengths to accommodate German demands.

In September 1940 Hitler took the decision to call off the negotiations. The Administrative Council was dissolved, and all political parties banned except the

Norwegian Nazi party known as *Nasjonal Samling* (National Unification), NS. Terboven proclaimed the King and government to have been deposed, their places taken by a new Cabinet dominated by NS members and responsible to the Commissar. NS and Quisling were given the chance to carry out a national-socialist revolution.

Throughout the war, Norway played an important part in German military strategy. Hitler once spoke of the country as a place of destiny where the outcome of the war might be decided. He feared an Allied invasion on his northern flank, and therefore built strong defences along the entire coast. At its maximum the occupation force numbered 430,000 men. Norway was an important deployment area in the campaign against the Soviet Union, and the Germans also launched fierce attacks on the north Atlantic convoy routes from air and naval bases in Norway.

The German armament industry made extensive use of Norwegian metals. The aircraft construction industry was assured supplies of aluminium and magnesium, while ammunition factories were well provided with pyrites. The Germans also seized control of much of the country's fresh fish and the production of canned fish.

The occupation years were characterised by political suppression and brutality unparalleled in modern Norwegian history. About 2000 members of the Resistance lost their lives after the end of hostilities in 1940. More than 30,000 individuals were imprisoned, and about 8000 sent to concentration camps in Germany. Among these were 760 Jews, of whom only 25 survived. Slave labour camps were established for Russian, Polish and Serbian prisoners-of-war, and in them both German and Norwegian Nazis could give vent to their racist tendencies. Over 17,000 prisoners perished. They died of malnutrition, disease and maltreatment, and many were executed.

Collaboration with the Germans

In the 1930s the causes of support for National Socialism were first and foremost economic crisis, fear of Communism, and dissatisfaction with parliamentary democracy. When in the course of the war the Norwegian Nazi party NS was given its historic opportunity, around 55,000 joined it. Many of these were convinced of the rightness of participating in the fight against the Communist Soviet Union, and that Germany would emerge victorious. About 7000 Norwegians served on the German eastern front, and between 800 and 1000 of them lost their lives there. When the Nazis took over national and local government, some public-office holders chose to become members of NS to keep their jobs. As for young people, the party's radical programme appealed to some, while others joined the party because their parents did.

However it was not only members of NS who collaborated with the Germans. Many companies accepted assignments from them, and thousands of workers were employed on German construction sites. More than 9000 Norwegian women gave birth to babies fathered by German soldiers.

Resistance in Norway

When NS took over the entire political scene in the autumn of 1940, Quisling made it his goal to gain control of the public administration. He also intended to take over the nation-wide organisations and, in line with the fascist model, subordinate them to a National Assembly. Another of his aims was a Norwegian-German peace treaty which would assure Norway a place in a new «Greater Germanic» Europe. His plans included establishing a new Norwegian army which would be brought into the war on the German side.

This attempt at Nazification was a fiasco, mainly because Quisling struck the bedrock of Norwegian democracy. Once people realised that the most fundamental human rights were at risk, a broadly-based opposition movement came into being. In the autumn of 1940 the Supreme Court resigned. The committee of the Sports Association stood down, and sports clubs protested against Nazi reorganisation of the country's sports by boycotting all official sports meetings. The bishops were

Opposition to the Germans and NS was expressed in many odd ways. This front page of Norsk Ukeblad *pokes fun at Hitler's help for Quisling. It resulted in the editor being sent to a German concentration camp.*

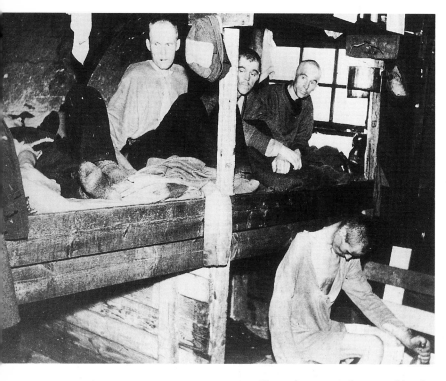

In 1945 there were over 100,000 Slav prisoners-of-war in Norway. Many of them were in a pitiful state when the war ended.

Children of Norwegian Nazis were often forced to join the «Children's Hird». Many of them suffered insults and beatings.

next to repudiate the new rulers, and in the spring of 1941 several professional and trades associations did the same. In September of that year Terboven declared a state of emergency in Oslo in order to put an end to the civil resistance. Two trade union officials were shot, and the leaders of the Federation of Trade Unions and the Employers' Confederation were replaced by NS members. As a result, there was an exodus from the Nazified bodies and clandestine ones were formed instead.

Civil resistance peaked in 1942. Teachers refused to join a Nazified teachers' union, and tens of thousands of parents buried the authorities in letters of protest. They would not accept pupils being organised in a national-socialist youth movement. The Germans countered with mass arrests of teachers, but this simply intensified opposition, and NS was forced to abandon its campaign in the schools.

Gradually a resistance leadership evolved which established close links with the government in exile in London. Towards the end of the war this leadership succeeded in preventing young Norwegians being summoned to do labour and military service for the Germans. Thus Quisling's

hope of forming a new national army was extinguished.

Not until the final phase of the war did the military aspect of the resistance come to predominate. Building up a secret army, *Milorg,* capable of effective action against the mighty German war machine, took time. At first many feared German reprisals. Weapons and equipment had to be smuggled in from abroad, and recruits had to be trained.

In 1943 the Resistance leadership coordinated civil and military resistance, and *Milorg* achieved mutual trust and cooperation with both the government in exile in London and the Allied military command. In 1944 and 1945 the so-called Home Forces carried out several acts of sabotage against railways and fuel stores. However, such attacks never became the most characteristic feature of the military resistance. Allied orders were that *Milorg* should be prepared for the eventuality of an invasion. This policy was criticised by the Norwegian Communists. They favoured guerrilla warfare and carried out a series of acts of sabotage on their own initiative.

Resistance Abroad

London became the headquarters for all
Norwegian resistance efforts abroad. The
Nygaardsvold government immediately
requisitioned the Norwegian merchant
fleet, and gathered it into «the greatest
shipowning company in the world», *Nortraship*. The ships were deployed to transport all manner of supplies for the Allies,
and became a life nerve for Great Britain.
But this had its price: 570 ships were sunk,
and over 4500 seafarers lost their lives.

The seafarers lived in constant fear.
They knew a torpedo could submerge their
ship. And that a tanker with a cargo of
petroleum could any moment become a
flaming inferno. The crews of ammunition
ships were no better off. They were fully
aware that being hit by a torpedo nearly
always meant a deadly explosion.

The income from this shipping activity
enabled the government to establish military units. Norwegian naval vessels participated in the sea battles in the Atlantic
and the North Sea. Pilots were trained in
Canada, and took part in the air battles
over Britain and the Continent. Army
units were organised in Scotland and
Sweden, to be deployed if Norway was
invaded. The government supported the
resistance movement with money, arms
and equipment, and attached great importance to keeping up morale both in Norway
and abroad. In addition to the government's endeavours came the great contributions made by King Haakon and Crown
Prince Olav. Tirelessly they travelled
about, encouraging seafarers and troops.
Their radio broadcasts boosted the morale
of the nation back home. And they
championed the cause of Norway with the
Allies.

The Liberation

The population in the north of Norway
was hardest hit by the events of the war.
The towns of Bodø and Narvik were severely damaged in 1940, and eastern Finnmark

county was subjected to heavy bombing by
the Russians in 1944.

In the autumn of 1944 the Soviet Union
gained the upper hand in the north, and
the Germans were forced to withdraw from
Finnmark and the northern part of Troms
county. On their way south the Germans
burned to the ground over 10,000 buildings
and destroyed thousands of boats, roads,
bridges and quays. Nothing of any value
should be left for the Red Army. The inhabitants were forced to flee.

In the spring of 1945 there were still
some 360,000 Germans in Norway. Vast
destruction and loss of life were feared if
they refused to surrender. Thus it was to
everyone's great relief that the Germans
laid down their arms without a fight on 8
May 1945.

With peace came an extensive judicial
process against those who had collaborated with the enemy. Almost 53,000 were
tried and convicted of treason, and some
23,000 of these received prison sentences.
Quisling and 24 other Norwegians were
executed. And 12 Germans were shot in
Norway for war crimes.

*The German «scorched
earth» tactics in Finn-
mark and northern
Troms in autumn 1944
caused serious pro-
blems for the civilian
population. This fami-
ly made a temporary
home in a ruined boat.*

The Resistance Movement

When the Germans invaded in 1940 they demanded an end to all opposition, and acceptance of a German occupation. These demands were refused by the King and the government. The fighting in southern Norway lasted three weeks, but the struggle continued in the Narvik area until 7 June. Then the government and the royal family crossed to London to carry on the war.

In Norway the Germans set about reorganising the country along Nazi lines with the help of Vidkun Quisling and NS. But this was thwarted by people in the worlds of sport, the Church, education and various trades and professions who combined into a broadly-based resistance movement. Towards the end of the War the resistance leadership cooperated closely with the government in exile in London to form a clandestine army, Milorg. In May 1945 the Germans laid down their arms, and on 7 June the King and the government returned to a liberated Norway.

Norwegian merchant seamen operating on all the seven seas made Norway's most significant contribution to the Allied victory over Hitler's Germany. 570 ships were sunk and over 4500 men lost their lives.

King Haakon and Crown Prince Olav were the most powerful symbols during the struggle against the German and the Norwegian Nazis. The photograph shows them during an air raid near Molde in April 1940.

A soldier of the Norwegian brigade during exercises in Scotland. In 1945 the Norwegian army in Great Britain numbered about 4300. The navy had 51 vessels and about 7500 men.

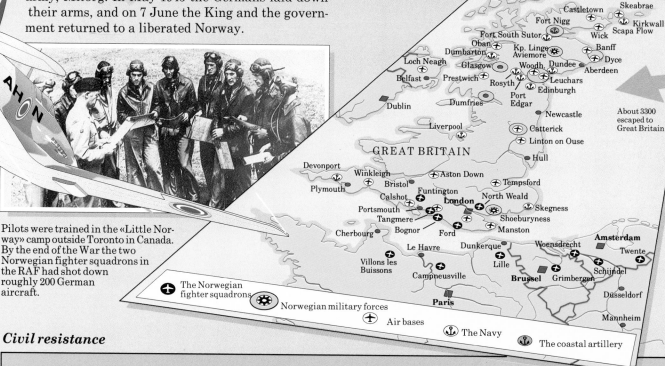

Pilots were trained in the «Little Norway» camp outside Toronto in Canada. By the end of the War the two Norwegian fighter squadrons in the RAF had shot down roughly 200 German aircraft.

About 3300 escaped to Great Britain

GREAT BRITAIN

⊕ The Norwegian fighter squadrons

⚙ Norwegian military forces

✈ Air bases

⚓ The Navy

⚓ The coastal artillery

Civil resistance

Sports

In the autumn of 1940 the Nazis disbanded the sports clubs and associations and replaced them by a new Department of Sport and Labour Service. Young Norwegian sportsmen and women protested. They refused to take part in competitions held by the new, Nazi association. The public boycotted Nazi sports meetings. Many athletes organised illegal sporting events. Often the members of the banned sports clubs would become the nucleus of the local branch of the military resistance, Milorg.

The Church

In the spring of 1942 the bishops and almost all the clergy in the Church of Norway resigned from their official state positions in protest at the Nazification process. Parish work was continued clandestinely. The photograph shows a Nazi church service, with just one person in the congregation.

The Schools

1100 teachers were arrested in 1942 and 650 of them sent to do forced labour in Finnmark county because they refused to join their Nazified union.

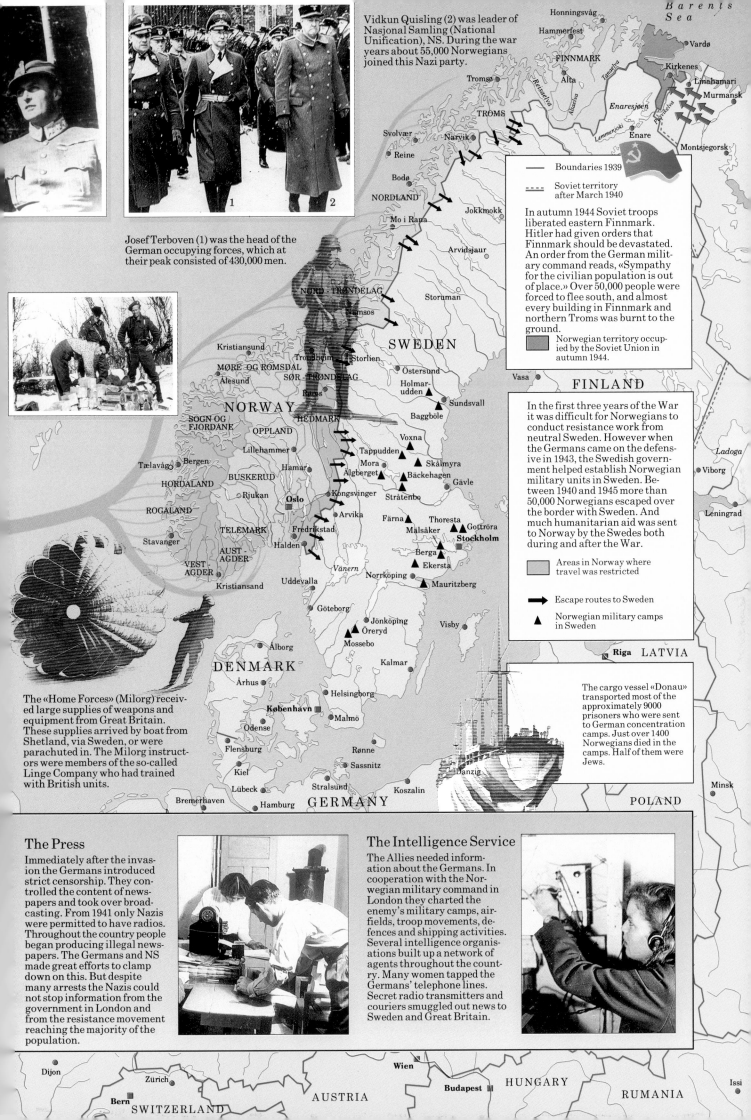

Vidkun Quisling (2) was leader of Nasjonal Samling (National Unification), NS. During the war years about 55,000 Norwegians joined this Nazi party.

Josef Terboven (1) was the head of the German occupying forces, which at their peak consisted of 430,000 men.

— Boundaries 1939

---- Soviet territory after March 1940

In autumn 1944 Soviet troops liberated eastern Finnmark. Hitler had given orders that Finnmark should be devastated. An order from the German military command reads, «Sympathy for the civilian population is out of place.» Over 50,000 people were forced to flee south, and almost every building in Finnmark and northern Troms was burnt to the ground.

Norwegian territory occupied by the Soviet Union in autumn 1944.

In the first three years of the War it was difficult for Norwegians to conduct resistance work from neutral Sweden. However when the Germans came on the defensive in 1943, the Swedish government helped establish Norwegian military units in Sweden. Between 1940 and 1945 more than 50,000 Norwegians escaped over the border with Sweden. And much humanitarian aid was sent to Norway by the Swedes both during and after the War.

Areas in Norway where travel was restricted

Escape routes to Sweden

Norwegian military camps in Sweden

The cargo vessel «Donau» transported most of the approximately 9000 prisoners who were sent to German concentration camps. Just over 1400 Norwegians died in the camps. Half of them were Jews.

The «Home Forces» (Milorg) received large supplies of weapons and equipment from Great Britain. These supplies arrived by boat from Shetland, via Sweden, or were parachuted in. The Milorg instructors were members of the so-called Linge Company who had trained with British units.

The Press
Immediately after the invasion the Germans introduced strict censorship. They controlled the content of newspapers and took over broadcasting. From 1941 only Nazis were permitted to have radios. Throughout the country people began producing illegal newspapers. The Germans and NS made great efforts to clamp down on this. But despite many arrests the Nazis could not stop information from the government in London and from the resistance movement reaching the majority of the population.

The Intelligence Service
The Allies needed information about the Germans. In cooperation with the Norwegian military command in London they charted the enemy's military camps, airfields, troop movements, defences and shipping activities. Several intelligence organisations built up a network of agents throughout the country. Many women tapped the Germans' telephone lines. Secret radio transmitters and couriers smuggled out news to Sweden and Great Britain.

THE PERIOD AFTER 1945

Cooperation and Solidarity

On 7 June 1945, five years to the day after King Håkon VII had been forced to flee the country, he landed once again on Norwegian soil. When the King who had been the symbol of unity in the long struggle for freedom and democracy stepped ashore on the quay in Oslo, it seemed that the cheering and rejoicing would never end.

Little did the King realise that the tall, thin man who greeted him in front of the new City Hall would come to symbolise the cooperation and welfare policies of the post-war years. When Einar Gerhardsen resigned as Prime Minister in 1965, he had become the «father of the nation» and one of Norway's greatest statesmen.

The resistance movement had brought people closer together during the war. The enormous reconstruction effort increased this feeling of solidarity, which was most clearly expressed in 1945 when all the parties stood for election on the same political platform. Their «Joint Programme» was obviously social-democratic in nature and showed that the Labour Party had achieved ideological supremacy.

The Joint Programme gave the state the main responsibility for social development and laid the foundations for the mixed economy on which Norwegian economic development has been based since 1945. In cooperation with private business and industry, the state would provide the necessary conditions for strong economic growth, which would ensure the population an improved standard of living and greater security. The Joint Programme also emphasised the fight against unemployment and the eradication of inequalities in living standards.

As in most other European countries, the war had radicalised the Norwegian population. At the 1945 election, the Labour Party achieved a clear majority in the Storting and was therefore able to form a government without having to seek the support of other parties. Apart from three weeks in 1963, the Labour Party remained in power for the next twenty years.

The Active State

In order to accelerate reconstruction, the Labour Party wished to utilise the exper-

Improvised children's procession in May 1945.

Opposite page: Labour Party election poster, 1945. It clearly shows that the party intended to build more power stations and create new industry to get the country on its feet again.

Einar Gerhardsen wanted dialogue with the Soviet Union. Here he is meeting Nikita Kruschev in Oslo in 1964. In the photograph on the right Gerhardsen is wearing his walking clothes. The Prime Minister went out walking or skiing in the hills and forests as often as he could.

ience gained from the British and American war economies. These countries had introduced centralised planning to produce weapons and equipment in the fight against fascism. Would it be possible to use similar methods to achieve the main goals of the Joint Programme?

These ideas were significant, as the new government was resolved to retain a large degree of government control of business and industry. The rationing system remained in force and the strict regulation of foreign trade, prices and wages continued. All construction and repair work had to be approved by the public authorities, who could also decide what was to be produced by industry. These inroads into the freedom of the private economy were accepted so long as they were necessary for the reconstruction effort, but when the government proposed legislation to continue its control of the economy after the

reconstruction period was over, battle commenced.

In 1953 the Labour Party was forced to withdraw these proposals, not least due to strong opposition from the non-socialist parties, the Federation of Norwegian Industry and other influential organisations. In the following years, the Party chose to cooperate with business and industry on the basis of mutual trust rather than to seek confrontation.

Soon after the war, the Labour Party pioneered the establishment of large, state-owned industrial companies. The most important of these were the iron works in Mo i Rana and the aluminium works in Årdal and Sunndalsøra. Such measures were never a main pillar of Labour industrial policies, however. Government support for private business and industry was more significant. The 1951 Plan for North Norway and the establishment of the Regional Development Fund in 1960 are good examples of this. Through these measures the government transferred large sums of money to the outlying regions. Agriculture and the fishing industry also received subsidies through separate agreements between the government and the farmers' and fishermens' organisations.

Although business and industry were given a freer hand in the 1950s, this did not mean that the Labour Party had given up the desire to steer economic development. In order to achieve this, the Party employed the services of expert economists, not least Minister of Finance Erik Brofoss. He sought the advice of Ragnar Frisch and Trygve Haavelmo, both later to win the Nobel Prize for Economics. Both the Cabinet and the Storting had to attend courses to learn about recent economic theory, with its hundreds of new terms and phrases. To start with the economists were met with scepticism. Conservative C. J. Hambro, for example, believed that they with their new tribal language, «the learned abracadabra», were being unleashed on a «defenceless society».

The Members of the Storting felt fairly helpless when Brofoss presented the new economic theories in his famous Budget Speech of 1946. After a few years, however, both the National Budget and the long-term plans were accepted by all the political parties. The main employers' and workers' organisations also appointed their own economists, who to a large extent cooperated with government economists.

With the help of this new expertise, the government wished to obtain a full picture of the country's labour force, raw materials and means of production. It also wanted to see the Norwegian economy as a coherent whole. What effects did the activities of private and public companies have on Norway as a whole? How could the Budget be utilised to achieve the main aims of the Joint Programme? These were the kinds of questions to which the economists hoped to find the answers in their calculations.

Aluminium production in Årdal, 1948.

In the late 1950s, the Labour Party relied increasingly on this macroeconomic control of the economy. Direct government intervention in individual companies had to make way for indirect methods. The government used taxes and duties to influence demand and production. For example, it introduced high taxes on motor cars to save foreign exchange. Subsidies in the Budget kept food prices low so that wage demands would not be too high. Interest rates were kept at a low level so that investments in business and industry would increase. This shows that the Labour Party did not want the government to get too closely involved in the private market economy. It preferred to ensure that the market functioned as well as possible.

While employers were given a freer reign, the Labour Party retained its influence over the trade union movement. The leadership of the Norwegian Federation of Trade Unions helped to ensure modest wage claims and prevent strikes. However, the trade union movement had little reason for complaint as long as conditions for the workers continued to improve.

Stability

During the 1950s and 1960s there was little variation in the relative strengths of the political parties. This political stability was founded on the spirit of cooperation that remained from the war years and the reconstruction period. Norway benefited from the international economic upswing. The mass unemployment of the inter-war years was over, and most of the population experienced increasing prosperity and security. This meant that the main goals of the Joint Programme had been fulfilled and the Labour Party was given the credit.

The broad agreement on growth and welfare policies shows how ideological differences between the parties diminished. Some people even maintained that the old ideologies were dead and the party programmes had become tame, with no broad perspectives. One radical critic of the Labour Party expressed his desire to go back to inter-war slogans, like «Down with the altar, the throne and the money-bags!», which had some bite. He did not think much of the 50s slogan «Solidarity for peace and progress!» and said it was «round as a bun, soft and cosy as an eiderdown. It might as well say «Happy Christmas and a prosperous new year!».

However, this criticism was atypical and had little effect. Both the Labour Party and the non-socialist parties were moving towards the centre to attract the most rapidly-growing electoral group – the white-collar workers. One sign of this was that the Farmers' Party changed its name to the Centre Party in 1959.

One important reason for new political stability in the post-war years was the growth of the *corporate system*. The government and the administration worked in close cooperation with the various pressure groups organisations and these non-governmental organisations were consulted on matters which affected them. They were allowed to comment upon proposals for legislation and participated on official boards, committees and councils. In this way the Norwegian Shipowners' Association, for example, had a considerable influence on Norwegian shipping policy, while the farmers' organisations managed to persuade the government to protect agriculture by means of high customs duties and import restrictions. In many cases the Storting chose to rubber stamp solutions which the experts in the administration and the organisations had agreed beforehand. A number of questions which could have caused serious conflict were therefore withdrawn from party political debate.

In contrast to the inter-war years, the period after 1945 was characterised by broad agreement on defence and foreign policies. As the temperature in the cold war dropped, fear of the Soviet Union grew, and the Labour Party joined the non-socialist parties in a common front against the Norwegian Communists. This truce also contributed to improved cooperation on domestic matters.

Orientation towards the West

«Today it is Czechoslovakia, tomorrow it may be Finland's turn, (......) it may be a matter of life and death for us all».

This statement from the Storting in February 1948 clearly shows that the optimistic hopes for peace of the days of the liberation were soon replaced by a new fear of war. When the Communists seized power in Czechoslovakia, and the Soviet Union demanded bases in Finland, the alarm bells rang in Norway. Foreign and defence policy would have to take a new course.

In the first years after the liberation, Norway had relied on the ability of the new world organisation, the UN, to ensure peace. The government wanted to build bridges between nations. Norway would avoid block politics and stay out of military alliances. At the same time, everyone agreed that the nation's defence should be strengthened.

The foundations of this «bridge-build-ing» policy soon began to crumble. A deep division arose between East and West in 1947. The Soviet Union tightened its grip on Eastern Europe, while the USA promised military and economic aid for countries that felt threatened by the Soviet Union. Cooperation between the super-powers in the UN stagnated. The «Cold War» had begun.

In this situation, Norway was too weak, both economically and militarily to play an active mediating role. The country was Norwegian policy in the UN was therefore passive and careful.

After the liberation of Finnmark, most Norwegians had great sympathy with the Soviet Union, but by autumn 1946 attitudes had already begun to change. When Norway's powerful eastern neighbour demanded Norwegian-Soviet military bases on Spitzbergen, there was deep suspicion. The government rejected this demand and increased the military cooperation with the western powers which had never been officially terminated at the end of the war. The majority of Norwegian weapons were purchased in Britain and from 1947 Norway took part in

Trygve Lie was Minister of Foreign Affairs from 1941 to 1946, when he was elected the first Secretary General of the United Nations. At the beginning of the 1960s he became Minister of Trade, and later Minister of Industry.

the occupation of Germany under British command. At the same time, ties were strengthened with the British and American secret services.

Norway took an important westward step in 1947, when the government decided to take part in the Marshall Plan. It was an easy decision. Norway's most important trading partners did the same and there was an acute lack of foreign exchange.

The coup in Czechoslovakia early in 1948 led to an intense anti-communist campaign. Prime Minister Einar Gerhardsen took the lead in the crusade against the «enemy within». The Norwegian Communists were now regarded as Soviet fifth-columnists who «in their hearts» were «supporters of terror and dictatorship».

The Norwegian Communist Party (NKP) had recruited new supporters during the war. Because of its active efforts in the resistance and its new social-democratic peace programme, the NKP won 11.9 percent of the vote at the 1945 general election. But the NKP did not manage to maintain this position for long. As early as 1946, the Labour Party, under its Secretary

Haakon Lie, had begun to register communists and remove them from responsible positions in the trade union movement. The anti-communist campaign led to mass desertions from the Communist Party, and internal disagreements weakened it. The situation was not made any easier by the fact that the NKP supported the Soviet Union in the Cold War and chose a more revolutionary course. In a short time the Party was reduced to a small, isolated sect in Norwegian politics.

When the confrontation between East and West grew more serious in 1948, there were negotiations between Norway, Sweden and Denmark for a Scandinavian defence union. These negotiations were unsuccessful. The Swedes wanted an independent alliance, while Norway wanted to have ties to the West through arms purchase agreements and clear guarantees of support in case of war, which had to be prepared in peace-time.

After the breakdown of the Scandinavian talks, more and more people felt that only membership of NATO would provide Norway with the necessary security. For a long time there was considerable scepti-

The head of Milorg, Jens Christian Hauge, was Minister of Defence from 1945 to 1952. Here he is seen at Sola Airport near Stavanger in 1951, receiving new fighter planes from the USA. On Hauge's left, Commander-in-Chief, General Dwight D. Eisenhower. The officer standing behind Hauge is General Lauris Norstad, who was Chief of the US Air Force in Europe.

cism about this within the Labour Party but when the Prime Minister overcame his doubts, his opponents fell into line. In spring 1949 the Storting passed by a large majority a resolution to join the new western alliance.

After joining NATO, the government took steps to reassure the Soviet Union. The so-called Bases Declaration laid down that Norway would not allow foreign troops or atomic weapons to be based on Norwegian territory in time of peace. In subsequent years there were also restrictions on military activities in Finnmark. This policy was intended to prevent the Soviet Union from increasing its pressure on Finland.

At the same time, Norway wanted to show her willingness to defend herself. The defence budget was increased, and both the conscript army and the military reserve were expanded. The bases policy did not prevent NATO forces from taking part in exercises of short duration on Norwegian territory. The army also established early warning systems and built up stocks of weapons for allied reinforcements. The headquarters of the NATO Northern Command was located in Oslo.

In the 1950s, Norway gave higher priority to cooperation with the USA and Britain than with the Scandinavian countries and Western Europe. Economic policies were coordinated within the Organisation for European Cooperation (OEEC), which was working for free trade. Norway therefore had to allow more imports into the country and invest in goods and services which Norway had the natural resources to provide, such as aluminium and shipping.

Norway rejected plans for a Scandinavian customs union and was critical of the EEC. Norwegian business and industry feared competition from Swedish industry and Danish agriculture. Many Norwegian politicians were also sceptical about supra-national organisations. It was not until 1960 that Norwegian industry made serious attempts to compete on an international scale. Norway then joined the west-

European, British-dominated European Free Trade Association, EFTA. This organisation reduced customs duties between member states, but had no supra-national authority, no common external customs barriers and did not include agriculture and fisheries.

Norwegian troops took part in the occupation of Germany between 1947 and 1953. The photograph shows a soldier who has just arrived in Schleswig in 1948.

Defence

King Christian IV established a Norwegian army in 1628. From 1750 onwards officers were trained at the Military Academy in Christiania. Most of the crew of the Danish-Norwegian fleet were Norwegians.

After 1814 Norway had her own defence forces and when the union with Sweden was dissolved in 1905 the country had a strong defence.

Defence was neglected after the First World War. When the Germans attacked in 1940, the country had little possibility of defending itself. Norway became a member of NATO in 1949. The Norwegian defence system has always been based on a popular army. All males were still conscripted for national service in 1990.

When a man was conscripted everyone on the farm had to help. Men and servarts forged and sharpened weapons, while women sewed clothes and prepared food for one to two months.

Akershus Castle in Oslo, about 1300

THE NAVY

King Hans founded a joint Danish-Norwegian fleet in 1510. Today the Coastal Artillery is an important element in naval defence.

King Christian IV's warship «Den norske løve»

«Løvendahls galle 1712

THE ARMY

Foot soldiers have always been the backbone of the Norwegian popular army. Up to 1854 only farmers were conscripted into the army.

Conscription was a system of defence that was used both on land and at sea. The farmers supplied ships, crews, soldiers and food. The king organised the conscription system.

Conscript ship

King Håkon V (1299–1319) built more fortresses than any other king, including Akershus, Vardøhus and Båhus castles.

Norwegian infantry soldier, early eighteenth century.

Ski divisions were first established in 1720, two in the north and two in the south.

Ski soldier, 1800.

Farming families sought refuge in local forts in times of war. The forts were built in locations that were easily defended. When the enemy approached, the farmers lit fires (beacons) on the tops of hills to warn people in the neighbouring settlements.

«*Start*», built in 1912, was Norway's first aircraft. The aircraft was donated to the Navy by people who had collected money for it. In June 1912 Lieutenant H. F. Dons completed the first flight in Norway, across the Oslo museum of Science and Technology from Vestfold to Østfold. The aircraft is on exhibition at the Norwegian Technical Museum in Oslo.

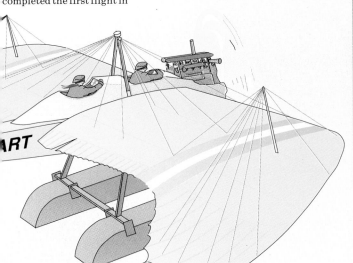

Defence in peacetime

In peacetime there are about **41,000** staff and forces. 27,000 of these are on national service.

 Air Force **10 500**

 Navy **7900**

 Army **22 000**

Prof. staff **500**

 Civil Defence **500**

Civil Defence

The Civil Defence is a civilian organisation within the defence system. The task of the Civil Defence is to reduce losses and damage as far as possible in case of war.

THE AIR FORCE The Army and the Navy established their own air forces during the First World War.	Fokker, 1929–1940	Spitfire of the Second World War	Vampire, the Norwegian Air Force's first jet fighter, 1948	Sabre, 1950s	F-16, 1980s
...nes, c. 1800	Monitor «*Mjølner*», c. 1900	Gunboat, 1905	The destroyer «*Sleipner*», 1936–1957	Motor torpedo boat of the 1970s	Modern coastal fort	Missile gunboat «*Odd*» of the 1980s
...riksten fortress ...alden	Norway increased its defences in connection with the Union conflict with Sweden. In the period up to 1905 strong border defences were built from Halden to Kongsvinger.	Cavalryman in the 1930s.	Sten gun of the Second World War	Leopard tank of the 1970s	Soldier from the Brigade in northern Norway.	UN soldier

...is soldier of 1905 was equipped with a Norwegian-produc-...Krag-Jørgensen rifle. It ...s one of the best hand-held ...apons in the world.

Mobilised soldier of 1990 in full field equipment with an AG-3 rifle.

Mobilisation forces
Total strength 440,000

Air Force **37 000**

Navy **33 000**

Army **165 000**

Civil Defence **80 000**

Home Guard **90 000**

Industrial Guard **33 000**

State Railways **2000**

From 1929 there were women volunteers in the armed forces, called *lotter*. Today they do medical and welfare work. KIF (Women in Defence) was established in 1957.
Women joining KIF were obliged to serve if the forces were mobilised. They had no weapons training.
In the 1980s women became entitled to the same military training as men. Today there are women in all branches of the armed services. Equality between the sexes is more advanced in Norway than in any other European NATO country. The illustration shows a woman infantry soldier on a winter manoeure.

SAS opened its first air route between Scandinavia and New York in 1946. The airline was the first to begin flights between Europe and Japan over the North Pole in 1957.

A new Socialist Alternative

In the 1950s there was a clear majority for membership of NATO, although there were still small groups within the Labour movement who continued to fight it. They protested against rearmament and were dissatisfied with the way in which the leadership of the Labour Party tried to prevent free discussion on foreign and defence policy. They also disliked the fact that the Labour Party had become less socialist and more cooperative towards private business and industry.

At the end of the 1950s, the opponents of NATO had a new lease of life. Many of them were actively involved in the western European campaign against nuclear weapons. When the Labour Party Congress accepted the presence of nuclear weapons on Norwegian territory if there was a danger of war, they had had enough and formed a new party, which was called the Socialist People's Party (Sosialistisk Folkeparti).

The SF party programme showed that the old ideas of neutrality and disarmament dating from the inter-war years were not dating dead. Norway now had an offshoot of the «New Left».

To everyone's surprise, SF managed to win two seats in the Storting at the 1961 general election. The Labour Party therefore had a new, troublesome rival on the left wing.

Scandinavian Cooperation

Although the attempts to create a Scandinavian customs union and a Scandinavian defence alliance had failed, ties between the Scandinavian countries became stronger after the war. In 1962 the national assemblies of Sweden, Denmark, Iceland and Norway resolved to establish a new organisation, which Finland joined three years later. The Nordic Council consists of members of national assemblies and governments who meet once a year to discuss matters of common interest. The Council may not pass binding resolutions, but the recommendations of the Council have usually been implemented. In the 1950s passports were no longer required for travel between Scandinavian countries and a common labour market was established. The Council's main significance is nevertheless as a body where Scandinavian politicians can meet to exchange ideas and experiences.

Cross-border contacts between organisations and public authorities in Scandinavia also increased dramatically after 1945. The trade union movement is one example. When new reforms were to be introduced, it became normal practice to seek advice from sister organisations in neighbouring countries. During labour conflicts these organisations would also usually provide funds.

The Scandinavian countries cooperated closely in the UN. Small countries were more easily heard when they joined forces and agreed on common views.

Norwegians became more familiar with other Scandinavian countries in their spare time. In the 1950s increasing numbers made their first journeys abroad to Sweden and Denmark. After 1960 the Scandinavian countries exchanged television programmes and it became easier to receive broadcasts from across the border.

The Scandinavian Airlines System, SAS, was established in 1946 with the Swedish, Danish and Norwegian governments as the main shareholders. The company was a success, but did not become a model for future Scandinavian projects.

Norway and the Third World – from Kerala to NORAD

Norway has long had close ties with the third world. Norwegian merchant ships have been calling at overseas harbours since the 1700s, and the first Norwegian missionaries went to Asia and Africa in the early nineteenth century.

Norway was one of the first countries to introduce bilateral development programmes. In 1952 the Storting allocated funds for a Norwegian-Indian fishery project in Kerala. The initiative came from the leadership of the Labour Party, who wanted to

Calling at overseas Marit Blengsli worked for the Norwegian Volunteer Service in Kenya. At the end of the 1980s over half the volunteers were women and more than half the projects were providing aid for women and children.

distract the opponents of Nato members-hip. However, when the Storting planned the first development aid programmes other considerations were of greater importance. Many politicians were interested in using development aid to stop the tide of Communism, while others were concerned to show Christian charity and solidarity with their fellow men who lived in poverty.

In 1962, Aid to India was renamed Norwegian Development Aid. This organisation was retitled NORAD six years later (now the Norwegian Agency for Development Cooperation) and in 1984 came under the aegis of the new Ministry for Development Cooperation.

Norway was one of the countries that gave the most aid as a proportion of GNP. Approximately half these funds went to a number of extremely poor, priority countries in Asia and Africa. The rest was transferred to UN agencies and non-governmental, humanitarian organisations. In the 1980s Norway gave more aid per capita to the UN agencies than any other OECD country.

Norwegian development aid was intended to reach ordinary men and women in the countries concerned. It was given mainly in the form of gifts rather than loans and very little was tied to the supply of Norwegian goods and services. From the end of the 1970s, private business and industry became more deeply involved in the developing countries as a result of the Storting providing increasingly large export credits for companies exporting to those parts of the world.

Growth

From 1945 to 1990 the Norwegian population increased from 3.1 to 4.3 million. The mortality rate continued to fall and people lived longer. In 1989 the average life-span for women was 79.85 and for men 73.34 years. This was due to improvements in health services, diet and housing. New medicines were particularly important in eradicating infectious diseases, especially tuberculosis.

Although the population grew, the number of children declined. From the mid-1960s the birth rate sank dramatically with the introduction of new contraceptive devices and birth-control pills. For the first time, women were able to decide for themselves when and whether to have children. The fall in the birth rate was also due to more women being in employment or further education in the 1960s.

At the end of the war, many people believed that Norway would suffer a post-war depression, as had happened after the First World War, but 1945 saw the beginning of remarkable economic growth which would make Norway one of the richest industrialised countries in the world.

Reconstruction was achieved more rapidly than expected. Both the GNP and industrial production had exceeded pre-war levels by 1946 and until 1950 Norway's economic growth was the highest in Europe. The government utilised the rationing system to limit private consumption. Investments were to be aimed at production which would bring in foreign exchange. This meant that imports of ships and machinery had priority over bananas and private cars. Nevertheless, these controls did not prevent rapid growth in the consumer goods industry. The government was particularly unhappy about the mushrooming of companies producing decorative objects and toys.

The great demand for new production equipment from abroad led to an acute foreign exchange crisis in 1947. The American Marshall Plan was therefore a godsend. Norway received about US$ 400 million in Marshall Aid. This money was not only used for raw materials and machinery. The Americans arranged study tours to the USA so that Norwegian companies could learn about modern industrial technology and rationalisation. Cooperation in connection with Marshall Aid also laid the foundations for an official technical-scientific research fund and a Norwegian productivity institute. These measures contributed to increased industrial efficiency. Productivity was 70 percent higher in 1960 than in 1948.

Although productivity increased and investments reached record levels, the rise in Norwegian GNP in the 1950s was lower than in most other Western countries. One of the reasons for this was that certain industries were encountering increasing competition. As a member of the Marshall Plan organisation, the OEEC, Norway had to allow imports of foreign goods. This particularly affected the manufacturers of consumer goods who had flourished in the 1940s due to high customs barriers and import restrictions. Some companies also had to cut back because the demand for many goods had been satisfied. The scarcity of labour and of loan capital also hindered growth.

Shipping experienced a new boom in the period between 1945 and 1973. In 1968 Norwegian ships accounted for approximately 10 percent of the world merchant fleet. Over half of them were large tankers, but several shipowners also commissioned new specialised cargo ships, such as container ships and ships for transporting motor cars. The number of seamen reached new heights – about 57,000 in the mid-1960s. From then on, the number of seamen employed on Norwegian ships gradually fell, not least due to the rapid modernisation of the fleet.

Norway has supported free competition on the oceans of the world since 1945. Attempts by various countries to reserve freight for their own ships, or for those of their trading partners, has therefore always been strongly opposed by Norwegian shipowners and governments.

Reconstruction and Prosperity

The burned-out, ravaged areas of Finnmark and northern Troms had the highest priority in the reconstruction effort. The area was full of dangerous mines and it would take a long time before proper housing and the necessary supplies could be provided for the population. The authorities therefore decided that only men

capable of working would be allowed back in the first year. However, the homesickness of the evacuees was so acute that the prohibition on travel was a fiasco. In the summer of 1945 thousands of families left their temporary homes in the south and headed north. At first they lived in earth huts, wrecks, plank shacks and barracks. The majority did not move into permanent homes until the beginning of the 1950s.

In the 1950s great changes took place in the daily life of the people. A man who grew up outside Sarpsborg says:

«I was born in 1946, one of 70,727 Norwegian children, and am therefore a member of the largest group of children ever born

Norwegian labourers unloading goods received through the Marshall Aid programme.

Teenagers dancing to rock and roll at a youth club in Oslo, 1957.

Opposite page, top: In 1950 16 per cent of university and college students were women. After the mid-1980s more women than men were entering into higher education. These girls enrolled at the University of Oslo in 1958.

Opposite page; bottom: A worker at the enamel works in Hasle, Oslo, proudly demonstrating a washing machine, 1953.

bought land in the neighbourhood. With cheap loans from the newly-established Housing Bank they started to build their own houses. The sites were usually excavated with shovels and much of the building was a cooperative effort.

Like most other married women in the 1950s, my mother was a housewife. I remember well how delighted she was about all the new appliances that made the housework easier. When we could afford to buy a washing machine, mother no longer had to struggle with the boiler, washboard and sinks in the cold, damp cellar. The new refrigerator saved us children from long walks with the milk pail to the dairy. Now we began to buy bottled milk that did not turn sour in the summer heat.

Although we no longer had to have ration cards for chocolate, sugar, meat and coffee at the beginning of the 1950s, there were many goods that could not be found in the shops. We therefore squeezed into one of the few private cars that existed in the neighbourhood and headed for Strømstad in Sweden. The car belonged to an officer who had brought it home after attending a course in the USA. We felt like kings as we swept into the back yard with the Studebaker's trunk full of tins of pineapple.

It was easy to see the difference between people in the 1950s. The white-collar workers still had high status and on Constitution Day it was normal for those who had got into university to parade in their student caps. The workers went to work in overalls and the farm children smelt of cowsheds. Everyone dreamed of buying a new car, but most had to make do with a moped, a motorbike or an old, second-hand car.

Only a few of the kids at our school went on to secondary education. There was competition for the places and further education was expensive. Most people wanted to go out to work as soon as possible.

The USA was the great ideal for most of us. We both admired and copied the Americans and let ourselves be influenced without objecting. In the newsreels we saw how the USA was protecting us in the Cold War against the Soviet Union. In our games

in one year in Norway. Many people say that we were the result of the liberation celebrations.

When the war ended there was a desperate need for housing. My father was one of the lucky ones. He rented some rooms from a newly-rich packaging manufacturer who had bought the officers' mess in a German camp. I grew up there with my mother, father and sister.

Nearly all my friends lived in the German barracks on the other side of the road. While we had our own bathroom, with a lavatory, wash basin and shower, the barracks children had to make do with an outside lavatory, wash bowls, zink tubs and chamber pots. But their situation improved. In the early 1950s several of the barracks families *inspired by cowboy films we all wanted to be Roy Rogers or Hopalong Cassidy, but in the new comics the western heroes had to compete with Donald Duck and the other Disney characters.*

The blue jeans fashion affected all the teenagers. The boys abandoned their knee-breeches and the girls stopped wearing skirts. We wore Lees or Wranglers and liked to have a Camel in the corners of our mouths. We chewed flat, American chewing gum, drank Coca Cola and played rock and roll on the juke box. The future looked bright.»

Social Welfare

The war had brought people closer together. When it ended there was broad agreement that the class struggle, unemployment and social hardships of the inter-war years must not be allowed to return. Many of the ideas behind the new welfare state came from the British «Beveridge Plan». Now it was not only society's losers who were to receive assistance from the public authorities. All citizens would have the right to support when they got into situations that created insecurity and financial need.

Since the country's economy was improving, the Storting had the opportunity of creating a finer-meshed social security network. Child benefits were introduced in 1946, giving all parents with children under 15 a fixed, monthly sum from the state. In the 1950s health insurance became compulsory and there was no longer a means test to qualify for an old-age pension. The protection of workers and children improved. New measures were also implemented to help the mentally retarded, people with occupational injuries and the mentally ill. In 1964 the Act relating to Social Welfare imposed new responsibilities on the municipal social welfare offices. They were not only to support the needy, but ensure that people became able to help themselves.

The most comprehensive social reform came into force in 1967. The National

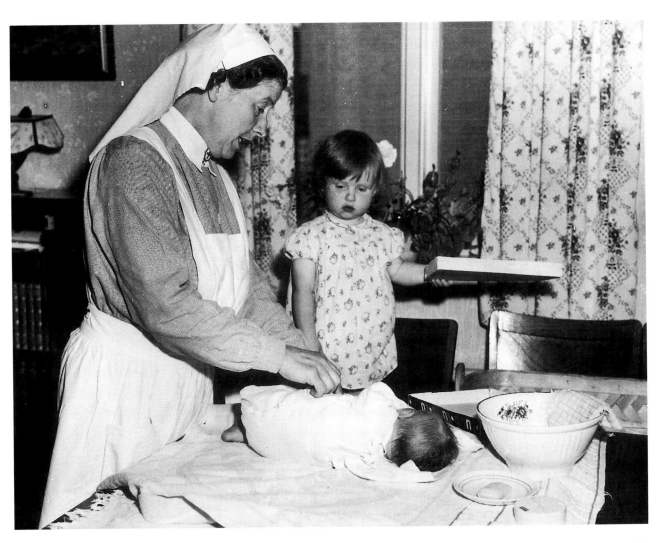

From the 1950s families where the housewife was ill could get help from municipal home helps.

Insurance Act ensured that most of the old insurance schemes were coordinated. It guaranteed all citizens support in old age, during illness and in the case of disability or unemployment. It also guaranteed assistance to pregnant women and people who had lost one wage-earner. The Act also covered the divorced, separated and single parents.

Both employers and employees had to contribute towards financing the National Insurance scheme. However, their contributions were not sufficient to cover costs and the National Insurance allocations in the Budget increased dramatically.

In the 1960s and 1970s the health service had highest priority. The 1969 Hospitals Act made the counties responsible for constructing and running hospitals, while the state provided most of the financing.

The municipalities built old-people's homes and employed home-helps and nurses to care for the elderly.

The costs of health and social welfare programmes accounted for an increasing proportion of public expenditure and the number of employees in the welfare state grew rapidly. At the end of the 1970s, most people thought that social distress and poverty had been eradicated for ever, but in the decade that followed there were indications that thousands of people were living in «invisible poverty».

Christianity, Contraception and Abortion

There were disagreements on cultural policy in the post-war years, too. In matters related to philosophy of life and sexual morality the conflict stood particularly between the Labour Party and the Christian Democrats. Soon after the liberation, the Christian community made strong attacks on the government for funding information on contraception. It was regarded as particularly reprehensible that such assistance was given to unmarried women.

When the government later agreed to the distribution of condoms to soldiers in the brigade that was stationed in Germany, a new battle began. In a nation wide protest action the Christian community managed to collect over 440,000 signatures against the plan. The government did not give way: the Labour Party did not accept the premise that this measure could undermine sexual morality. It regarded it as more important to limit venereal disease and unwanted pregnancies.

The Christian community received more support for its views when the Labour Party presented plans for reductions in religious education in primary schools. Over 750,000 people protested against the proposal and the plans were shelved as a result of the biggest ever signature campaign in Norway.

The abortion question also raised tempers. The Labour Party's women's organisations reiterated their demand of the interwar years for a new abortion law that would allow abortion on social grounds. Although the number of illegal abortions increased in the 1950s, the men in the Labour Party leadership would not support the women's proposal. The new Abortion Act of 1960 showed clearly that the government had bowed to the demands of the Christians and the doctors; neither low income, bad housing nor other social conditions were regarded as good enough grounds for abortion. Hospital doctors were given absolute authority to grant or deny abortion applications.

The Abortion Act created discontent and the abortion conflict flared up again in the 1970s.

In the 1960s and 1970s many companies invested in aluminium manufacturing. This kettle was produced at Nordisk Aluminium in Holmestrand.

A happy Fredrikstad family with a new Ford Consul in 1960. At the beginning of the 1960s most cars were imported from Britain. German and Japanese cars later took over most of the Norwegian car market.

The Affluent Society

«New inventions, new methods of production and new raw materials open unknown opportunities for increasing our prosperity (.....) We must carry out a policy which will enable our country to utilise these technical advances (.....) Then we can meet the future with confidence and optimism».

This quotation from the 1957 election campaign can serve as an example of the belief of most people in economic growth. There was also optimism about prosperity in the 1960s. Only at the end of that decade could an increasing number of warning voices be heard, critical of the detrimental effects of growth. But before these criticisms entered into the debate, the country experienced an amazing upsurge in prosperity.

The period from 1960 to 1974 was a gold-

en age for industry, which took advantage of the expanding international economy and succeeded in the hard competition brought about by free trade between EFTA countries. Foreign investments increased, particularly in the energy-intensive industries. At the end of the 1960s Norway had become the biggest exporter of aluminium in Europe and the biggest exporter of ferro-alloys in the world.

Most companies which had traditionally produced for the domestic market proved to be capable of selling their products abroad. The mechanical engineering industry did particularly well, as did the furniture and printing industries.

Strong industrial growth led to expansion in the retail trade and the transport and construction sectors. It was therefore not surprising that there was a growing demand for manpower. Luckily there was a reserve available. In the 1960s an increasing number of married women went out to work. Many people wanted higher incomes to buy new material goods. It was also easier to go out to work, because women were having fewer children than before.

The private car was a symbol of the new prosperity. From October 1960 it was no longer necessary to apply for permission to buy a car and in subsequent years thousands of proud car-owners were soon driving along Norwegian roads. Demand did not fall although the number of traffic accidents increased dramatically.

Nearly all the machines that were installed in the new power stations after the war were produced in Norway. Between 1950 and 1980 hydro-electric power production increased by more than 500 per cent. In the 1980s Norway had the highest per capita consumption of electricity in the world. The photograph shows a generator being installed in the Aurland power station at the beginning of the 1970s.

From Chamonix...

The Olympic rings symbolise the five continents, and the Olympic Games aim to promote fraternity and friendship among all the world's peoples. Winter Olympics were first held in 1924 at Chamonix, France. Since then they have been organised for the same years as the Summer Olympics.

Norwegian sportsmen and women have traditionally done well in the Winter Olympics. Up to 1988 they had achieved a total of 165 medals: 54 gold, 57 silver and 54 bronze. In recent years the competition has intensified and at Calgary in 1988 Norway for the first time failed to win a single gold medal.

In 1952 Norway hosted the 6th Winter Olympics, in Oslo. 1178 competitors from 30 countries competed in 22 events.

When Lillehammer was allocated the 1994 Winter Games, the organisers determined to produce a sporting occasion which would accentuate delight in sport and the environment. Many of the country's outstanding athletes have links with Lillehammer. Haakon Brusveen, Simon Slåttvik and Brit Pettersen, all of them skiers and Olympic gold medallists, are examples. Most of the events will take place at Lillehammer, but neighbouring towns will also share in hosting the Games. Hamar will have a new skating arena, and some of the ice hockey matches will be played at Gjøvik.

THORLEIF HAUG was one of the best Norwegian skiers of all time. In 1924 he not only earned gold medals in the 50 km Cross-country and the 18 km Cross-country but also was winner of the Nordic combined event and bronze medallist in the 90-metre hill Ski jump.

SONJA HENIE was the star name in the sporting world during the interwar years. She was Olympic figure skating champion in 1928, 1932 and 1936; she also won nine World Championship titles and six European titles.

HOLMENKOLLEN was the principal arena for the Nordic skiing events in the Winter Games of 1952. The ski jump was originally built in 1892 but has been altered several times since.

STEIN ERIKSEN won a gold medal in the Giant slalom in the Winter Olympics of 1952. Two years later he achieved three gold medals in the Alpine-skiing World Championships. In 1954 he turned professional and thereafter skied in the USA.

BISLET STADIUM was the venue for the speed skating events in the 1952 Olympics. HJALMAR ANDERSEN (known as «Hjallis») won gold medals in the 1500, 5000 and 10,000 metres. He won the World Championship titles in 1950, 1951 and 1952.

LAKE PLACID 1932

BIRGER RUUD is Norway's greatest ski jumper ever. He won Olympic gold medals in 1932 and 1936 and a silver medal in 1948, besides being World Champion in 1931, 1935 and 1937.

GARMISCH - PARTENKIRCHEN 1936

IVAR BALLANGRUD is the Norwegian speed skater with the largest number of Olympic medals. In 1936 he won gold medals in the 500, 5000 and 10,000 metres, and a silver in the 1500 m. He had already won a gold medal in the 500 m and a bronze in the 1500 m in the 1928 Winter Olympics, and a silver in the 10,000 m in 1932.

HALLGEIR BRENDEN won gold medals for the 18 km Cross-country skiing event in the 1952 Olympics and the 15 km in 1956. He was also in the relay teams which won silver medals in the Winter Games of 1952 and 1960.

OSLO 1952

CORTINA 1956

INNSBRUCK 1964

TORALF ENGAN won an Olympic gold medal in Ski jumping (80-metre hill) and a silver medal in the 70-metre hill event, both at Innsbruck in 1964. In 1962 he was World Champion (70-metre hill).

MAGNAR SOLBERG was Olympic champion in the 20 km Biathlon in both 1968 and 1972, the first Biathlon competitor to win two Olympic gold medals. He was also in the Biathlon relay team that earned a silver medal in 1968.

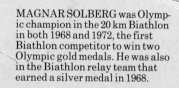

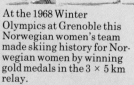

GRENOBLE 1968

INGER AUFLES, BABBEN ENGER AND BERIT MØRDRE

At the 1968 Winter Olympics at Grenoble this Norwegian women's team made skiing history for Norwegian women by winning gold medals in the 3 × 5 km relay.

SAPPORO 1972

...to Lillehammer

The winter sports town of Lillehammer at the northern end of Lake Mjøsa has the honour of organising the Winter Olympics for 1994.

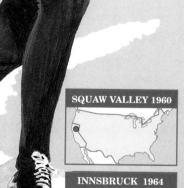

SQUAW VALLEY 1960

INNSBRUCK 1964

LAKE PLACID 1980

KNUT JOHANNESEN was nicknamed «Kuppern» by the Norwegian speed skating crowds. He won Olympic gold medals in the 10,000 metres in 1960 and the 5000 m in 1964; silver medals in the 10,000 m in 1956 and the 5000 m in 1960, and a bronze medal in the 10,000 m in 1964. «Kuppern» was World Champion in 1957 and 1964.

BJØRG EVA JENSEN was the only Norwegian to win a gold medal at the 1980 Winter Olympics. It was in the 3000 m Speed skating.

LILLEHAMMER 1994

Nyksund in Norland, one of the many coastal fishing settlements abandoned in the 1960s and 1970s.

Centralisation

Although Norway did not experience the same expansion of urban areas as took place on the continent, there was nevertheless a mass movement of population after 1945. At the end of the war about half the population lived in towns and communities with over 200 inhabitants. Twenty-five years later this figure had increased to about two thirds. This did not lead to whole districts becoming depopulated, as happened in Sweden and Finland. The women in the areas people were leaving had more children than other areas and most of those who left settled in a larger town in the same district.

Those who moved further mainly chose to go to the south-east. Most of them came from northern Norway and the west coast. They were in the main young people under 30 and the majority were women.

Many mountain, forest and valley communities were seriously affected by this migration, but the coastal municipalities north of Trøndelag were the worst hit. Typically, they all lacked industry and had bad communications.

This great migration must be seen against the background of far-reaching changes in agriculture, forestry and fishing.

From the 1950s agriculture was increasingly mechanised. The tractor replaced the horse for ever and animal husbandry became easier. Most farms had running water and electricity. In the course of a twenty-year period a centuries-long lifestyle disappeared, and the daily life of the farmers' wives changed radically. The old wood-burning stove ended on the scrap heap and new household appliances were brought into the kitchen. There was no more exhausting water-carrying, and the milking machines took over in the cow-

Haymaking the old and the new way on two farms in Rogaland, 1964.

shed. Agricultural labourers had to find new work and there was no longer much need for help from female farm labourers and youngsters during the harvest. Many farmers gradually took on paid employment as well as running the farm.

Combine harvesters replaced the old threshing machines, and the use of feed concentrates, silage, pesticides and artificial fertilizers increased rapidly. The farmers also acquired improved breeds of animals and plants. They also continued to build up the agricultural cooperatives all over the country so that farmers shared the purchase, production and sale of goods and services. The results that were achieved in milk production aroused particular attention. With the help of breeding and feeding experiments, Norwegian cattle became among the most productive in the world.

The farmers managed to persuade the majority of the Storting to pass laws to protect agriculture against foreign competition. The politicians also agreed to provide large agricultural subsidies. This was done to reduce depopulation, but also to prevent the country from becoming too dependent on imported food. Norway had the lowest proportion of domestic supply of agricultural products in Europe and most people believed that the modest area under cultivation (about 3 percent) should be maintained. In the case of war or crisis it was important that the best farms should be kept intact.

Although nearly half of all Norwegian farms closed down between 1945 and 1975, the area under cultivation was not greatly reduced. The most resilient farms took over land from the farms that closed down and the clearing of new land continued. All the same, much good agricultural land was lost due to the expansion of urban areas. Most of the farms that survived specialised in corn, dairy farming or livestock production.

New techniques affected forestry too. Hard labour with axes, hand-held saws and barking spades came to an end. The foresters now used motor saws and bark-

ing machines. Less timber was floated down the rivers and lorries took over the transportation of timber to sawmills and pulp and paper factories. Mechanisation led to the loss of thousands of jobs in the forestry industry.

In the 1930s Norwegian fishermen had managed to get a law introduced forbidding the building of new trawlers. They feared that modern fishing boats would put them out of work during a period of high unemployment. The situation was different after the war. The politicians agreed that fishing had to be rationalised and catches should be sold to the filleting factories, refrigeration plants, fish-meal plants and fish-oil factories to increase the country's export earnings. The fish processing companies wanted – and got – reliable supplies from new trawlers which went far out to sea and ensured year-round supplies of raw materials.

Work in the fisheries became easier and less dangerous in the first decades after the war. There was new machinery for hoisting the modern purse seine nets on board. Echo-sounders and sonar made it easier to find the fish, and weather forecasts were more reliable. New nylon and plastic gear saved the fisherman from lifting heavy loads.

The modernisation of the fishing industry led to a steady drop in the number of fishermen. Those who left the profession were mainly combined farmer-fishermen and many of them also chose to leave their smallholdings.

New technology led to bigger catches than ever before. But could the fish stocks stand the strain? By the 1960s there were signs that they could not.

The development of communications was also instrumental in determining where people would live and work. Although the railway to the north was extended as far as Bodø and electric trains replaced the old steam locomotives, roads had the highest priority. The main roads were asphalted to carry the heavy lorries which took over much of the transportation of goods from railways and ships. The num-

ber of lorries rose from 21,000 in 1950 to 70,000 in 1975.

The construction of new airports was particularly important in the 1960s. On demostic routes SAS had to compete with other airlines for passengers, the two most important being Braathens SAFE and Widerøe. By the mid-1970s the airlines were carrying nearly four million passengers a year.

Many of the outlying areas that were affected by depopulation did not benefit from the improvements in communications. People in these areas found that ferry and bus services were disappearing, or that the railway station and the post office closed down. Automation of the telephone network also led to a loss of jobs for many women who had worked at the old telephone exchanges.

Norway had 744 municipalities at the end of the war. Twenty years later this number had been reduced by three hundred, since many municipalities had been merged. New roads had often made the old municipal boundaries irrelevant and many of the smaller municipalities did not have the financial resources to carry out all the tasks imposed on them by central government. They had to develop schools and run social welfare offices and engineering services. New legislation obliged the municipalities to plan housing, industrial areas, water supplies and sewage pipelines.

The amalgamation of local authorities led to intense conflicts in many local communities. It was particularly difficult to decide where the new administrative centre would be located, and with it the most jobs and the best services.

Most of the railway system was electrified in the first 25 years after 1945. Here the old meets the new at Nelaug station on the southern region railway in 1949. The last steam engines were taken out of service in 1970.

Agriculture

After 1660 farmers were able to buy the land they farmed and most of them became freeholders. The population increased and in many areas farms were divided up, particularly on the west coast. The cottar system appeared at the same time. The number of cottar families increased until the mid-nineteenth century. At that time there were 67,000 cottars in Norway, but from then on the numbers declined. Many emigrated to America or found work in the towns.

After 1850 there were great changes in agriculture. Farmers had better technical equipment and sold their produce in the towns. Many farms specialised in corn production, dairy farming or livestock production.

Summer farm

The farmers built summer farms in the mountains and on summer pastures. The women stayed there to milk the cows and make butter and cheese.

Cottars

The cottar's family cultivated a piece of land at the edge of a farm. Prior to 1850 the family could be moved from the land at the farmer's whim.

Large farm of the eighteenth century

On a farm like this the farmer's family worked with the help of many servants and cottars.

This women is milking a Telemark cow. Looking after the cows and milking were women's work.

Animal husbandry

Prior to 1850 farming families wanted to be as self-supporting as possible. They cultivated corn, kept animals, hunted, fished and picked berries. Dairy farming and livestock production had a special position on the farm – everyone needed milk, meat, wool and hides. However, dairy farming was not as profitable as it is today. In the 1700s a cow produced an average of 500 litres of milk per year, while today a cow will normally produce eleven times this amount. One important reason for the low production of milk was that cows had too little feed in winter and cow-sheds were narrow and dark.

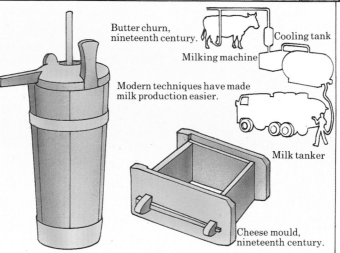

Butter churn, nineteenth century.

Milking machine

Cooling tank

Modern techniques have made milk production easier.

Milk tanker

Cheese mould, nineteenth century.

New technology.

In the latter half of the nineteenth century the wooden plough was replaced by the iron plough. Farmers bought new equipment such as sowing machines, harvesters, horse-drawn rakes and threshing machines.

The first dairies were established in the 1860s and by 1875 the country had about one hundred dairies and cheese factories. Farmers acquired new skills from agricultural colleges. In 1859 the Norwegian College of Agriculture was established at Ås in Akershus county. It was called the «Farmers' University». The use of artificial fertilisers increased after 1900.

Agriculture did well from 1900 to the 1920s. Many farmers borrowed money for new machines and buildings. The inter-war crisis seriously affected farming, however. Prices dropped and the farmers had difficulty in repaying their debts. Although many farms closed down after 1945, production increased.

In the 1980s only one in three farmers farmed full-time. Since 1950, subsidy agreements between the farmers and the government have ensured a good income for those working in agriculture.

Farmers own most of the forests in Norway. Income from forestry has always been important.

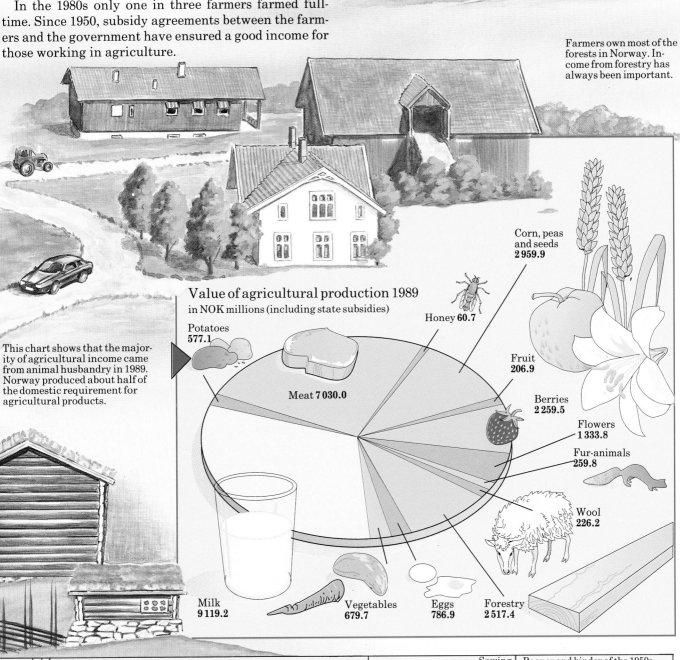

This chart shows that the majority of agricultural income came from animal husbandry in 1989. Norway produced about half of the domestic requirement for agricultural products.

Value of agricultural production 1989
in NOK millions (including state subsidies)

Potatoes **577.1**

Honey **60.7**

Corn, peas and seeds **2 959.9**

Fruit **206.9**

Meat **7 030.0**

Berries **2 259.5**

Flowers **1 333.8**

Fur-animals **259.8**

Wool **226.2**

Milk **9 119.2**

Vegetables **679.7**

Eggs **786.9**

Forestry **2 517.4**

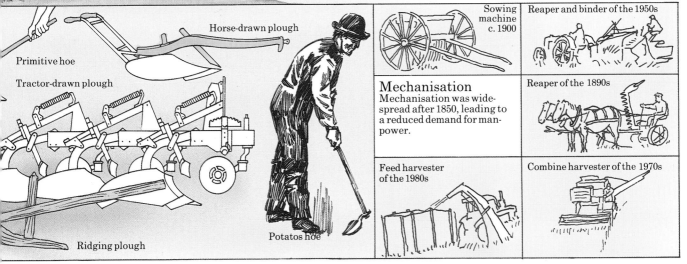

Primitive hoe

Horse-drawn plough

Tractor-drawn plough

Ridging plough

Potatos hoe

Sowing machine c. 1900

Reaper and binder of the 1950s

Mechanisation
Mechanisation was widespread after 1850, leading to a reduced demand for manpower.

Reaper of the 1890s

Feed harvester of the 1980s

Combine harvester of the 1970s

In 1963 the leader of the parliamentary Conservative Party, John Lyng, formed the first non-socialist government since the war.

The Non-socialist Takeover

After the 1965 general election, the four non-socialist parties, Conservatives, Liberals, Centre Party and Christian Democrats, were able to form their first majority government since the war. This was not the result of a steady effort in opposition. The four parties did not manage to agree on a vote of no confidence in the Labour Party government until 1963. Prior to this they had been unable to present a clear alternative government to the electorate. The prime reason for this was that the Labour Party pursued moderate, centrist policies, making it unnecessary for the non-socialists to close ranks.

In this situation the non-socialist parties found it necessary to emphasise the differences between them and preserve the old dividing lines. The Christian Democrats in particular were concerned to

demonstrate their uniqueness. The Party presented itself as a new, national, non-socialist alternative in 1945. It wished to be a guardian of Christian morality with a «message from God» – above class struggle and party political wrangling. Both the Liberals and the Centre Party were concerned about the numbers of supporters they lost to the Christian Democrats. It was difficult to cooperate when they were competing for the same votes.

The Centre Party defended the interests of the outlying regions and the farmers and often came into conflict with the Conservatives, who represented the culture of the towns and had close contacts with shipping and industry. The Liberals were split into a social-liberal and a liberalistic wing. The social-liberals made the running in the 1950s. They sympathised with the Labour Party's economic policies and were sceptical about the Christian

Democrats' views on cultural issues. At the beginning of the 1960s the question of Norwegian participation in the EEC also created difficulties for cooperation among the non-socialist parties. The Conservatives were advocates of full membership, the Centre Party was against and the Liberals and Christian Democrats were divided. Only after President de Gaulle of France had vetoed an expansion of the Common Market in 1963 were the parties able to join forces against Labour.

At the 1961 election the Labour Party and the non-socialist parties had an equal number of representatives in the Storting. The new radical left party, the Socialist Peoples' Party (SF) had won two seats. The Labour Party government would therefore have to resign if SF and the non-socialist parties were to agree on a vote of no confidence. This is what happened in 1963, when Labour Party industrial policy led to a non-socialist government. Firstly, the opposition attacked Labour for having provided millions of kroner in subsidies for a state company without the consent of the Storting. Secondly, they were dissatisfied that the government had not given the national assembly complete information about a mining accident in Kings Bay on Spitsbergen. In the opinion of the opposition, the Gerhardsen government had become self-willed and arrogant and therefore had to be removed.

Although the government led by John Lyng (Conservative) was voted out of office by the Labour Party and SF only three weeks later, it had a great psychological effect. The creation of a government had brought the non-socialists closer together and forced them to agree on a common political platform. At the 1965 election they achieved a majority of seats in the Storting and Per Borten (Centre Party) became head of a non-socialist, coalition government.

The Borten government followed the main policies drawn up by the Labour Party. The welfare state and other areas of public responsibility continued to expand. This cost money, and taxation in-creased. The non-socialist government brought in the National Insurance Scheme, compulsory nine-year schooling and the value-added tax.

However the Borten government was forced to resign in 1971. The coalition broke up during negotiations on Norwegian membership of the EEC. A minority government, led by Trygve Bratteli (Labour), managed to negotiate an agreement on full membership, but this was rejected by a national referendum in 1972.

The Education Explosion and the Revolt of Youth

From 1960, municipalities were given the option of introducing nine-year compulsory education. The old system, where secondary education was of two types *(real-skole and framhaldsskole)* was replaced by the new junior high schools *(ungdomsskole)*. In 1969 the Storting voted in favour of universal nine-year compulsory education.

The changes in basic education made it possible for increasing numbers of young people to enter into higher education. The number of pupils at senior high schools *(gymnas)* and vocational schools rose rapidly, and universities and colleges were swamped with new students. In 1968 new universities were opened in Trondheim and Tromsø and the establishment of regional colleges began in the following year.

Just like young people in other western countries, many Norwegian teenagers were highly critical of the prosperous adult society of the 1960s. The Anglo-American pop industry gained a solid foothold and provided the youngsters with new fashions and new ideals. Long hair and blue jeans were a sign that a separate youth culture was developing. Social contacts were freer and respect for all kinds of authority declined. Television gave the teenagers a new view of the world. They were the first to see in their sittingrooms live pictures of starvation and war. This media shock often caused

frustration and rootlessness among the young. Some of them reacted against the materialism and social climbing of their parents' generation.

In the mid-1960s hashish and marijuana were widely used in student circles. These drugs quickly became fashionable among the Norwegian hippies, whose main base was in the park outside the Royal Palace in Oslo. From here drug abuse spread to other groups of young people in the rest of the country.

When the universities became over-crowded, the authorities proposed that the old, open studies should be replaced by new curricula with fixed courses and more examinations. Behind this lay a desire to make the period of study shorter and better adapted to the needs of business and industry. The students went on strike and demonstrated to keep open the free studies, which gave room for social criticism. Inspired by the spirit of revolt at American and European universities, the students agitated against authoritarian university leadership and restrictive changes. Their

protests brought results. The students gained representation on the governing bodies of the universities and were consulted on the content of courses.

American invovement in Vietnam created sympathy for the cause of the developing countries. Many young people took the war as a sign that the rich countries had the main responsibility for the suffering and lack of freedom in the third world.

The most radical of the socialist students decided that the capitalist system in Norway should be overthrown by means of armed revolution. These Marxist-Leninists regarded Mao's China as their great ideal. In 1973 they formed a new Communist Party, AKP (m-l). In spite of the fact that the party was not represented in the Storting, they achieved influence in a number of local trade unions. They led several strikes and focused attention on work-places with low wages and bad working conditions. A number of young authors also joined the Marxist-Leninists, the best known of these being Jon Michelet and Dag Solstad.

A rock concert at Holmenkollen at the beginning of the 1970s.

A demonstration on International Women's Day, 8 March 1977.

In the 1960s more and more women entered into higher education. At the end of the decade the number of female students had reached about one third of the total. Female academics were also affected by the atmosphere of criticism and in 1970 some of them formed the first new-feminist group on the pattern of Women's Liberation, the American feminist movement.

The new feminist movement attacked the old sexual stereotypes which forced women to be passive and subordinate. Rebellious women formed small groups all over the country, with the main purpose of showing how women were suppressed in male society. They had plenty to do: men played a dominant role in politics and working life. Women often received lower wages than men for the same job. Married women complained about the lack of nursery schools and criticised their husbands for doing too little housework. Many also told of physical and mental violence in their marriages. All this led to thousands of women suing for divorce.

The Abortion Act of 1960 was another contentious point. The hospital doctors who ruled on applications for abortion did not follow a common practice, and illegal abortions could endanger women's lives. There were therefore new, forceful demands for women's right to self-determined abortion.

The Green Movement

During the 1960s it became apparent that powerful economic expansion had its drawbacks. Norwegian whaling in the Antarctic had to be stopped because too many whales had been caught. In the North Sea herring disappeared and the mackerel catch was greatly reduced. Emissions from industry, agriculture and sewage plants threatened life in lakes, fjords and rivers. Air pollution increased dramatically, acid rain from Great Britain and the Continent ruined thousands of fishing lakes in southern Norway and poisonous pesticides disturbed the natural ecological cycles.

The refuse tips expanded. So did the demand for electricity. The result was that an increasing number of waterfalls, rivers and lakes were regulated for hydro-electric power. The last wild, untouched areas in Europe were in danger of disappearing.

Pollution and the destruction of natural resources increased the influence of the

Emissions from smelting works were normal in the 1970s. This photograph shows Arendal smelting works in Eydehavn. In the 1980s the company invested millions to solve the problem, and the rest of Norwegian industry had to do the same.

environmentalists. The Norwegian Society for the Conservation of Nature headed the voluntary effort and demanded that the authorities should do something.

In 1962 the Storting passed a resolution to make the mountainous area of Rondane the country's first national park, and new areas were protected against exploitation in subsequent years. But the real breakthrough for environmentalism took place in the European Natural Conservation Year in 1970. In that year a new Nature Conservancy Act and a new Water Pollution Act were passed, and in the same year a group of environmentalists used civil disobedience for the first time in the struggle to protect the environment. They tried to stop a construction project to lead Mardalsfossen, the highest waterfall in Europe, through pipelines. The police removed the demonstrators, but they had managed to start a serious debate on the harnessing of waterways in general. In the 1970s the Storting passed resolutions to protect several waterways from regulation.

In 1972 the new Ministry of the Environment was given the main responsibility for government environmental and natural resources policy. Experts at the ministry prepared a mass of laws and regulations which contributed towards improving the

environment in many respects. But national measures alone were not enough. In the 1970s and 1980s Norway increased efforts to achieve international agreements on the environment.

The EC Struggle

Great Britain, Denmark and Ireland joined the European Community in 1972. Norway also negotiated a membership agreement, but this was rejected by a majority of the population in a national referendum. It therefore had to be replaced by a free trade agreement, which was signed in 1973.

Why were a majority of Norwegians against membership of the EC?

EC opponents were fiercely unwilling to give up Norwegian sovereignty to supranational bodies in Brussels. They were also against the EC's plans for economic and political union in Europe. This strong desire to retain national sovereignty must be seen aganist the background of centuries of union prior to 1905, when Norway was dominated by her Danish and Swedish neighbours. Many people were afraid that the country would once again be governed by remote control from a distant central authority. They also believed that demo-

Skiing in Rondane National Park.

cratically elected bodies had too little influence within the EC.

Many people objected strongly to the EC philosophy of growth. The principles laying down that goods, services, capital and labour should flow freely across national borders caused concern. Many people feared that European capital, particularly German capital, would dominate the Norwegian economy. This could lead to the depopulation of many outlying regions and increased pressure on Norwegian natural resources and the environment. The fear of such a development increased when the EC would not allow special measures to protect Norwegian farmers and fishermen.

Opponents of EC membership organised an effective popular movement which managed to win the battle for public opinion. Its principal elements were farmers, fishermen, left-wing socialists and radical trade unionists. They were also supported by many lay Christians, the temperance movement and adherents of the New Norwegian language.

The country's leaders supported membership. They stressed that the EC would strengthen the peace and create greater economic growth. They also emphasised that Norway would have more influence on developments in Europe as members of the Community than outside it. But these arguments from the majority of the Storting, headed by the Conservatives and the Labour Party leadership, did not carry enough weight, nor did the support of the biggest capitalists, the leadership of the Norwegian Federation of Trade Unions and most of the daily newspapers. A major-

ity of 53 percent voted not to join.

The EC debate created unrest in party politics. On the socialist side, the Labour Party lost support while the SF party (from 1973 SV) gained ground. A new, right-wing liberalistic party was formed, later to be called the Party of Progress. Norway's oldest party, the Liberals, were split and lost many voters. In 1985 the Liberal Party lost its last seat in the Storting.

At the 1973 and 1977 elections the left-wing socialists again held the balance of power between the non-socialist block and the Labour Party. As the largest party in the Storting, the Labour Party formed three minority governments in a row and sought support from different parties on an issue by issue basis.

When it was in power the Labour Party had to take into account the serious disagreements on norms and values that had arisen in Norwegian society during the EC debate. Many of the new reforms in the 1970s were a result of this debate. The successive Labour governments also had to respond to other challenges: Norway had to formulate an oil policy, ensure national control over large areas of ocean and strengthen the defence of the northern territories.

The Oil Revolution

Oil exploration in the Norwegian sector of the North Sea started in 1966. Many companies joined in the search for «black gold», but they gave up one by one. In autumn 1969 only Phillips Petroleum Company had not abandoned hope. In the last exploratory well the company had decided to drill, the Ocean Viking rig hit oil.

Demonstration against Norwegian membership of the EEC before the national referendum in 1972.

The gas flare on the Gulftide platform was lit in summer 1971, proof that Norway had become an oil-producing nation.

Margaret «Maggie» Knudsen was one of the women who began working in the oil industry in the 1980's.

Norway as an Oil Nation

In 1969 the Phillips Petroleum Company discovered oil on the Ekofisk field. The Storting decided that the state should play a key role in this new industry and Statoil was founded. The state company received large shares in new discoveries and became involved in the exploration, production and refining of oil and gas. Foreign companies and the Norwe-gian companies Norsk Hydro and Saga Petroleum also took part in the oil boom.

Oil activities also benefited Norwegian business and industry onshore. The petrochemical industry was established and the production of platforms and equipment brought increased employment. Oil production had its dangers, however. In 1980 the Alexander Kielland platform capsized and 123 people died. However this accident did not prevent exploration off the North Norwegian coast. The first promising gas discoveries were made on Tromsøflaket in 1981.

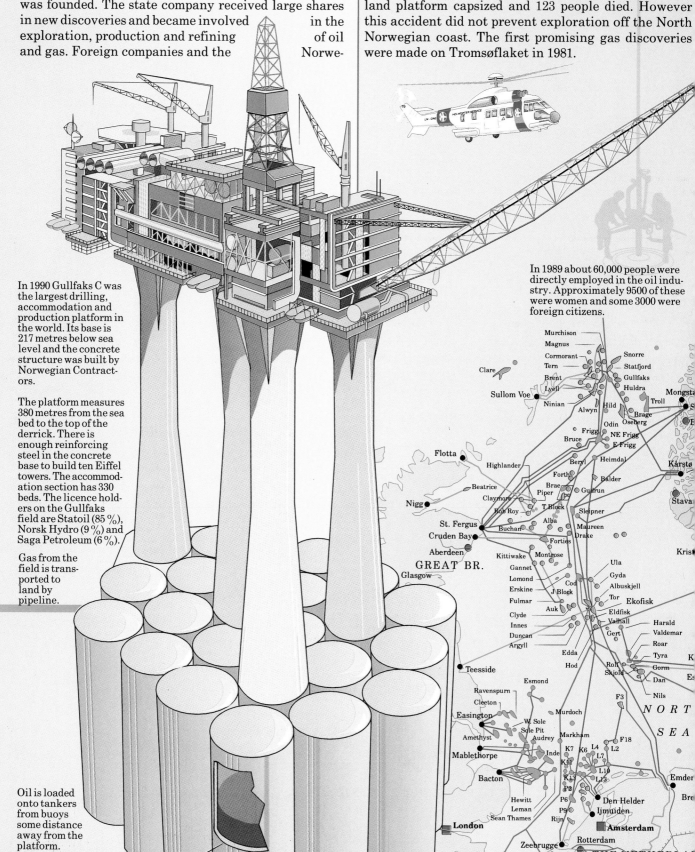

In 1990 Gullfaks C was the largest drilling, accommodation and production platform in the world. Its base is 217 metres below sea level and the concrete structure was built by Norwegian Contractors.

The platform measures 380 metres from the sea bed to the top of the derrick. There is enough reinforcing steel in the concrete base to build ten Eiffel towers. The accommodation section has 330 beds. The licence holders on the Gullfaks field are Statoil (85 %), Norsk Hydro (9 %) and Saga Petroleum (6 %).

Gas from the field is transported to land by pipeline.

Oil is loaded onto tankers from buoys some distance away from the platform.

The large underwater concrete cylinders are oil storage tanks.

In 1989 about 60,000 people were directly employed in the oil industry. Approximately 9500 of these were women and some 3000 were foreign citizens.

Murchison
Magnus
Cormorant
Clare
Tern
Snorre
Statfjord
Brent
Gullfaks
Huldra
Sullom Voe
Lyell
Ninian
Alwyn
Hild
Troll
Brage
Oseberg
Mongsta
Frigg
NE Frigg
Odin
E Frigg
Bruce
Flotta
Highlander
Beryl
Heimdal
Forth
Balder
Beatrice
Brae
Gullrun
Piper
Karstø
Claymore
T Block
Sleipner
Nigg
Rob Roy
Alba
Stava
St. Fergus
Buchan
Maureen
Cruden Bay
Drake
Aberdeen
Forties
Kris
GREAT BR.
Kittiwake
Montrose
Glasgow
Gannet
Ula
Lomond
Gyda
Cod
Erskine
Albuskjell
Fulmar
J Block
Tor
Ekofisk
Clyde
Auk
Eldfisk
Innes
Valhall
Harald
Duncan
Gert
Valdemar
Argyll
Roar
Edda
Tyra
K
Hod
Rolf
Gorm
Teesside
Skjold
Dan
Esmond
Nils
Ravenspurn
F3
Cleeton
Easington
Murdoch
NORT
W. Sole
SEA
Sole Pit
Amethyst
Markham
F18
Mablethorpe
Inde
K7
K6
L4
L2
L7
K11
L10
K13
L13
Bacton
P2
Hewitt
P6
Leman
P9
Den Helder
Sean Thames
Ijmuiden
Rijn
London
Amsterdam
Emder
Zeebrugge
Rotterdam
Bre
Dover
THE NETHERLA
Calais
Brussel
Köln
Lille
BELGIUM
Bonn
Le Havre
FRANCE
LUX.
Fra
Paris

0   200 km

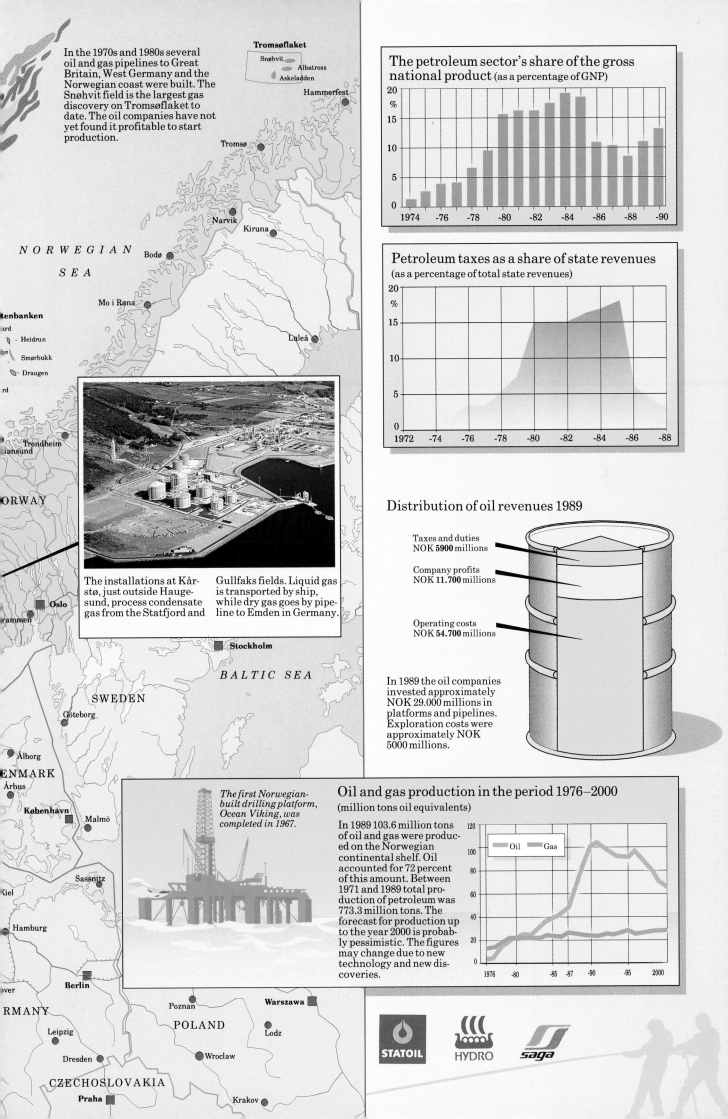

In the 1970s and 1980s several oil and gas pipelines to Great Britain, West Germany and the Norwegian coast were built. The Snøhvit field is the largest gas discovery on Tromsøflaket to date. The oil companies have not yet found it profitable to start production.

Tromsøflaket
Snøhvit
Albatross
Askeladden
Hammerfest

Tromsø

Narvik
Kiruna

NORWEGIAN
SEA

Bodø
Mo i Rana
Luleå

tenbanken
ard
- Heidrun
- Smørbukk
- Draugen
rd

Trondheim
iansund

ORWAY

Oslo
ammen

Stockholm

BALTIC SEA

SWEDEN
Göteborg

Ålborg

ENMARK
Århus
København
Malmö

Sassnitz
Kiel

Hamburg

Berlin
over

RMANY
Poznan
Warszawa
Leipzig
POLAND
Lodz
Dresden
Wroclaw

CZECHOSLOVAKIA
Praha
Krakov

The installations at Kårstø, just outside Hauge-sund, process condensate gas from the Statfjord and Gullfaks fields. Liquid gas is transported by ship, while dry gas goes by pipe-line to Emden in Germany.

The petroleum sector's share of the gross national product (as a percentage of GNP)

%
20
15
10
5
0
1974 -76 -78 -80 -82 -84 -86 -88 -90

Petroleum taxes as a share of state revenues (as a percentage of total state revenues)

%
20
15
10
5
0
1972 -74 -76 -78 -80 -82 -84 -86 -88

Distribution of oil revenues 1989

Taxes and duties
NOK **5900** millions

Company profits
NOK **11.700** millions

Operating costs
NOK **54.700** millions

In 1989 the oil companies invested approximately NOK 29.000 millions in platforms and pipelines. Exploration costs were approximately NOK 5000 millions.

The first Norwegian-built drilling platform, Ocean Viking, was completed in 1967.

Oil and gas production in the period 1976–2000
(million tons oil equivalents)

In 1989 103.6 million tons of oil and gas were produc-ed on the Norwegian continental shelf. Oil accounted for 72 percent of this amount. Between 1971 and 1989 total pro-duction of petroleum was 773.3 million tons. The forecast for production up to the year 2000 is probab-ly pessimistic. The figures may change due to new technology and new dis-coveries.

Oil Gas
120
100
80
60
40
20
0
1976 -80 -85 -87 -90 -95 2000

STATOIL
HYDRO
saga

Soviet forces on an exercise on the Kola Peninsula.

In 1970 the experts decided that the find was not only comercially viable, but that it was one of the ten biggest oil-fields in the world. Norway had become an oil-producing nation!

In the 1960 the Storting had passed legislation ensuring strict state control of – and high income from – oil activities. A special Oil Directorate, later to be subordinated to the Ministry of Oil and Energy, was responsible for implementing the new legislation. In order to ensure that Norway did not become only a raw-material exporter of oil and gas, the authorities decided to develop a national oil industry which would participate in exploration, production and processing of oil and gas resources in cooperation with foreign companies. The gigantic investments and high risk involved made it desirable to share the responsibility. The politicians gave the state oil company, Statoil, a preferential position with considerable shares in future discoveries, but the state-dominated Norsk Hydro and privately-owned Saga Petroleum were also allowed to participate.

The Continental Shelf and Pre-Stockage of Defence Equipment

As a result of the international conferences on the law of the sea in the 1970s, Norway was assured a continental shelf of approximately 1.5 million square kilometers and an economic zone of approximately 2 million square kilometers. No other European nation, with the exception of the Soviet Union, controls such a large area of ocean. The expansion of the offshore territory led to conflict with the Kremlin on boundaries in the Barents Sea. In the absence of a final solution a temporary agreement was signed on the distribution of fishery resources in the disputed area off the coast of Finnmark. Questions concerning the utilisation of offshore areas round Spitsbergen were not clarified, nor was it possible to reach agreement with Denmark on the boundary between Jan Mayen and Greenland. The latter conflict was referred to the International Court of Justice in The Hague.

The discovery of oil and new sovereignty over large offshore areas increased

US marines landing in Norhtern Norway during a NATO exercise in the 1980s.

Norway's economic and strategic importance. The growing Soviet military presence on the Kola Pensinsula had the same effect. In the 1970s the capacity of the Soviet Northern Fleet increased enormously. The ability of NATO to help Norway in case of war or crisis was once more on the agenda. This resulted in an agreement between Norway and the USA for pre-stockage of heavy weapons for an airborne marine infantry brigade in Trøndelag. Norway also signed an agreement concerning the establishment of support bases for American aircraft and naval vessels.

New Reforms

The EC conflict reflected much of the social criticism from the youth revolt and the green movement. After the national referendum, the politicians heeded the demands for democratisation, decentralisation and environmental protection, and oil revenues gave them improved opportunities for implementing reforms.

In 1972 the Storting passed an Act relating to industrial democracy which ensured that employees of large companies were represented on the board. They were also represented in the new corporate assemblies, which determined the main outlines of company policy. Five years later the

Storting replaced the old Workers Protection Act with a new Working Environment Act. This Act gave workers better protection against dismissal and stricter rules governing overtime and the working environment.

The winds of reform also reached the school system. This time the focus was on education for pupils between the ages of 17 and 19. A new, combined upper secondary school replaced the old *gymas,* vocational schools and business schools. After the Further Education Act was passed in 1974, combined schools grew up all over the

Russ celebrations, a Norwegian tradition marking the end of twelve years' schooling. This tradition has roots going back to the last century and did not die out when the upper secondary school took over from the old gymnas in the 1970s.

country and pupils were able to choose between more academic courses and practical, vocational subjects.

The EC conflict brought greater understanding of the problems of agriculture and the outlying regions. In 1976 the Storting passed a staged plan for farmers which ensured them higher incomes and proper holiday arrangements. The national assembly also passed laws allowing the transfer of a certain amount of authority from the central administration in Oslo to the counties and primary municipalities.

The new feminist movement increased its efforts to achieve equality between the sexes. The political parties had to ensure that women had more positions of responsibility and higher ranking on the party election lists. The number of women on representative bodies rose considerably. A milestone was rose in 1981, when Gro Harlem Brundtland became the country's first woman Prime Minister.

The Allodial Act (relating to the old system of land tenure) was amended in 1974, giving female and male heirs the same rights to inherit the family farm. The Equal Status Act came four years later and also contributed towards improving the position of women. It forbade sex discrimination and ensured equal pay for equal work. For example, employers were not allowed to differentiate between men and women when they employed, promoted or dismissed employees. An Ombudsman for Equal Status had the responsibility for ensuring that the new regulations were respected. The Act was followed up by several plans of action on equality in the 1980s.

The most important question for the new feminist movement in the 1970s was the demand for women's right to decide on abortion. The Christian movement rose up to fight for «the unborn life» and collected about 600 000 signatures in support of their

Tanker laid up at Karmøy, Rogaland, during the 1975 shipping crisis.

campaign. They had to give up, however. The Act relating to the Termination of Pregnancy was passed in 1978 with the support of the Labour Party and the Social Left Party.

A Period of Crisis, Oil Prosperity and Anti-Inflation Policies

The international economic recession caused by the oil crisis in 1973 led to a world-wide drop in production and widespread unemployment. Norway was an exception to the rule. The government used anticipated oil revenues to keep the wheels moving, taking up large foreign loans to help business and industry through the crisis.

The government also reduced taxes and expended large sums on new reforms. Between 1974 and 1977 real incomes increased and unemployment was held at bay. During this period Norway had a higher rate of growth than most other OECD countries, which proved to be a mixed blessing.

In 1977 the foreign debt had reached NOK 100 billion – over half the national product. At the same time Norwegian goods were losing in competition on world markets. The increase in wages and welfare had gone too far. Strong measures had to be introduced to reduce costs. The government reduced support to industry and shipping, introduced a wage and price freeze and devalued the krone. There were other problems, too. Norway was becoming increasingly dependent on oil revenues. Because of the instability of the price of oil, it was difficult to calculate government income.

The crisis in the 1970s affected shipping in particular. When oil prices rose, the demand for tankers fell. The majority of Norwegian shipowners had new, expensive ships which did not have long-term freight contracts. About half the tanker fleet was laid up. The problems spread to the shipbuilding industry. From the end of the 1970s many shipyards had to close down or adapt to new activities. Those

who invested in producing equipment for the new oil industry did best.

Many shipowners were close to bankruptcy. The government provided billions of kroner to prevent foreign shipowners from buying up parts of the fleet at depressed prices. The situation was not hopeless for all shipowners, however. Some managed to ride out the storm by investing in special bulk ships, cruise ships, oil rigs and supply ships for the oil industry.

A shipping crisis as serious as that of the 1970s would formerly have been a catastrophe for the Norwegian economy. Now, fortunately, large oil revenues could replace

Asylum-seekers in Østerdalen, summer 1990.

Sami people demonstrating against the development of the Alta Kautekeino waterway in 1981.

the foreign earnings lost in the shipping industry.

Immigration

The economic growth of the 1960s led to a manpower shortage, and for the first time for many years Norway had a surplus of immigrants. The majority of immigrants came from Western Europe and the USA. Many of them were experts in the oil industry. In the 1970s the number of immigrants from South-eastern Europe, Asia and Africa increased, not least because many West-European countries closed their borders to new immigrant workers.

The growing influx of unskilled labour from poor countries led the authorities to pass stricter immigration laws in 1975. Nevertheless, the number of foreigners continued to rise in the years that followed. The oil industry still needed skilled workers and many immigrants utilised their right to bring their families to Norway. In the late 1970s and early 1980s the country accepted several thousand Vietnamese refugees. Most of them had been picked up by Norwegian merchant ships in the South China Sea.

Immigrants from third world countries had difficulty in finding work and were more often affected by unemployment than

Norwegians. Although many of them were well educated, they usually had to make do with low-status jobs in the industrial and service sectors. They also lived in substandard housing.

Increased immigration tested Norwegian tolerance. People with little education and little experience of contact with immigrant workers were particularly sceptical. The most militant attacked immigrants' shops and spread racist propaganda. However, such groups never received widespread support. Both the authorities and the majority of the population were prepared to help the immigrants settle in Norway.

At the end of the 1980s a growing number of asylum-seekers from developing countries suffering from war and terror applied for asylum in Norway: almost 20,000 people between 1987 and 1989. It took a long time to process all the applications and the authorities had to provide temporary accommodation all over the country. Of the 3500 applications that were processed in 1987, approximately 75 percent were granted residence permits, mostly on humanitarian grounds.

Despite increased immigration, the Norwegian population is still very homogeneous, both ethnically and culturally, and immigration has been relatively modest. In 1987 only 2.6 percent of the population, approximately 115,000 people, were foreign nationals, compared with about 7 percent of the French and West German populations.

The Sami People Demand Their Rights

After the Second World War the authorities abandoned their hardline «Norwegianisation» policies and declared that they wished to protect the Sami culture, language and way of life. However, long as the Sami people had not organised themselves effectively and had no political leadership with clear-cut goals, the Norwegian authorities did little to implement the new policies.

There were several reasons for the Sami peoples' difficulties in organising themselves. They had been suppressed and dis-

criminated against for hundreds of years. Many of them had broken away from their Sami background and moved from the Sami districts. They were few in number, they were spread over four different countries and they spoke several different languages.

Rapid post-war industrialisation increased the pressures on the Sami populations. They were increasingly disturbed by the way the Nordic nations moved into areas where for thousands of years the Sami people had wandered freely.

When the State Power Authority wanted to develop the Alta-Kautokeino waterway their patience was exhausted. Under the slogan «Let the river live!» the Sami people and environmentalists joined forces to stop the bulldozers. Their campaign was supported by the indigenous populations of other countries and attracted international attention. In 1981 the

Kåre Willoch, leader of the parliamentary Conservative Party, being cheered by workers outside the Storting after the 1981 election victory. In the 1980s the Conservatives won votes from many traditional Labour supporters.

government sent a large police force to remove the demonstrators, and the construction of the power station could begin.

The Alta case forced the authorities to clarify the rights of the Sami people. One of the results of this was the establishment of a separate Sami assembly, the *Sameting*, in 1989. In the same year, the Storting amended the Constitution, to the effect that the Norwegian state was responsible for protecting the Sami language, culture and way of life.

The Swing to the Right

When Gro Harlem Brundtland took over as Prime Minister in 1986, eight women became Cabinet Ministers, a higher percentage of women than in any other government in the world.

After gaining the support of an increasing proportion of the electorate in the 1970s, the Conservative Party achieved its best ever election result in 1981. It received 31 per cent of the vote.

The progress of the Conservative Party showed that the swing to the right that could be observed throughout the western world had also reached Norway. However, there is no need to cross national borders to find the reasons. During the 1970s the Conservatives had established a powerful party organisation which recruited many new members. The Party demonstrated that it was capable of taking over most of the voters who had become rootless during the EC conflict. It was now easier for Labour Party former supportes to change to the Conservatives, who had a more social-democratic image. Moreover, these parties had cooperated closely in the effort to join the EC.

The reduction in the number of industrial workers, farmers and fishermen, the traditional supporters of the Labour Party and the Centre Party, was an advantage for the Conservatives. The Party also profited from the advance of urban culture and bourgeois values, while the class soli-

M/S Americana was the first combined crui- se and container ship in the world. The owners, A/S Ivarans Rederi, registered the ship in the Norwegian Interna- tional Ship Register (NIS). In spring 1991 over 900 ships were registered in NIS.

darity of the labour movement was losing ground. More people were moving into towns and built-up areas and the number of employees in white-collar jobs was in- creasing. The so-called anti-cultures – the temperance movement, Christian funda- mentalists and the New Norwegian lan- guage movement – were on the retreat and the Conservatives won the support of former Liberal and Christian Democrat voters.

The Willoch Period 1981–1986

After the 1981 election the non-socialist parties did not manage to form a majority government. Negotiations came to a halt when the Conservatives rejected a demand from the Christian Democrats to revoke the Abortion Act. The Conservatives there- fore formed a government alone, with Kåre Willoch as Prime Minister. The Christian Democrats took two years to recover from their defeat on the abortion question, but by the summer of 1983 their desire to be in power had returned and the Christian Democrats and the Centre Party joined the government .

The goal of Willoch's minority govern- ment was «to reestablish growth in the Norwegian economy». It reduced taxes, did away with several official controls and gave freer rein to market forces.

The authorities forfeited the right to impose ceilings on housing rentals and the members of most housing cooperatives were allowed to buy their own homes. The government also eased restrictions on the stock market. It became easier for foreign- ers to invest in Norwegian securities and there were tax advantages for people who bought shares in unit trusts. The turnover at the Oslo Stock Exchange quickly reach- ed record heights.

The non-socialist majority also agreed to dissolve the broadcasting monopoly. From 1982 new local radio stations were on the air and private companies started to develop cable networks for local television and satellite television broadcasts.

By the mid 1980s the government had managed to repay the foreign debt, but this was not enough to balance the economy. The number of unemployed increased steadily and in 1984 reached 80,000 or 5 percent, a new post-war record. Both the Labour Party and the centrist parties exerted pressure to increased public ex- penditure and thus reduce unemployment.

From 1985 the foreign debt increased again. At the same time, private consump- tion exploded. People bought new cars, video recorders, microwave ovens and other luxuries as never before. Most of this increased consumption was financed by bank loans. The banks also lent large sums to the retail trade and to speculators on the stock exchange and in the property business.

Norwegian Shipping

From 1850 to 1880 the merchant fleet increased substantially. In this third «golden age» Norway rose to third position among shipping nations. During World War I Norwegian vessels contributed to the Allied victory, at a loss of 2000 seafarers and half the fleet.

In the interwar period Norway acquired a modern fleet of tankers. At the end of the 1930s 60 percent of the total fleet consisted of motor ships, a higher proportion than in any other country. Following the German invasion of 1940, the Norwegian government in London requisitioned almost the entire merchant fleet. Norwegian seafarers sailed in the service of the Allies. 3400 of them died and nearly 3/5 of the fleet was lost. After 1945 came 30 years of continuous growth, but the 1970s saw a crisis in the world economy and half the tanker fleet was laid up.

As a result of high costs in the early 1980s, many shipowners registered their ships abroad. To revitalise Norwegian shipping the Storting passed the Norwegian International Ship Register (NIS) Act in 1987. In 1990 Norway's merchant fleet was once again the third largest in the world.

Norway's share of the world fleet

(ships over 100 grt)

Year	Norway grt	10	30	50	70	90%	World grt
1923	2 375 970						62 335 373
1928	2 953 944						65 159 413
1933	4 078 133						66 627 524
1938	4 613 175						66 870 151
1952	5 905 942						90 180 359
1958	9 384 830						118 033 731
1963	13 668 815						145 863 463
1968	19 667 441						194 152 378
1973	23 621 096						289 926 686
1978	26 128 428						406 001979
1983	19 229 966						422 590 317
1988	9 350 303						403 406 079
1989	15 596 900						410 480 693
1990	23 429 000	1990 estimate					423 627 198

SOVEREIGN OF THE SEAS

«Sovereign of the Seas» was built for Royal Caribbean Cruise Line in 1987. At 74,000 grt she was then the world's largest cruise ship and had a crew of 760. The ship accommodates 2600 passengers, and cruises in the Caribbean.

1 «Shipshape» keep-fit centre
2 Night club
3 Main lounge
4 «Music Man» cabaret/dance hall
5 Youth centre
6 Panorama lounge
7 Saloon
8 Casino
9 Restaurants
10 Champagne bar

Numbers employed in the Norwegian maritime community 1 January 1990

- Coastal trade
- International trade and the offshore industry
- Norwegians under foreign flag
- Shipowning companies and shipbrokers
- Shipyards and ship's equipment
- Finance, insurance, marine suppliers
- Auxiliary services

10 000
8 000
3 200
12 100
6 900
20 500
11 100

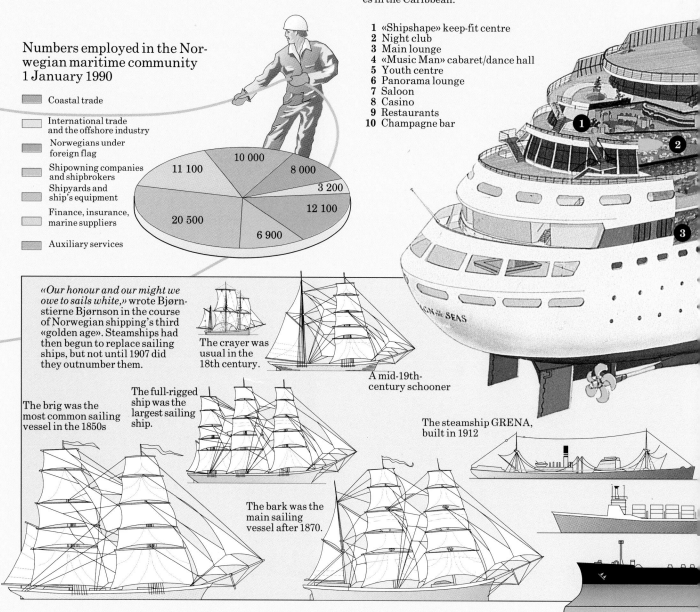

«Our honour and our might we owe to sails white,» wrote Bjørnstierne Bjørnson in the course of Norwegian shipping's third «golden age». Steamships had then begun to replace sailing ships, but not until 1907 did they outnumber them.

The crayer was usual in the 18th century.

A mid-19th-century schooner

The brig was the most common sailing vessel in the 1850s.

The full-rigged ship was the largest sailing ship.

The bark was the main sailing vessel after 1870.

The steamship GRENA, built in 1912

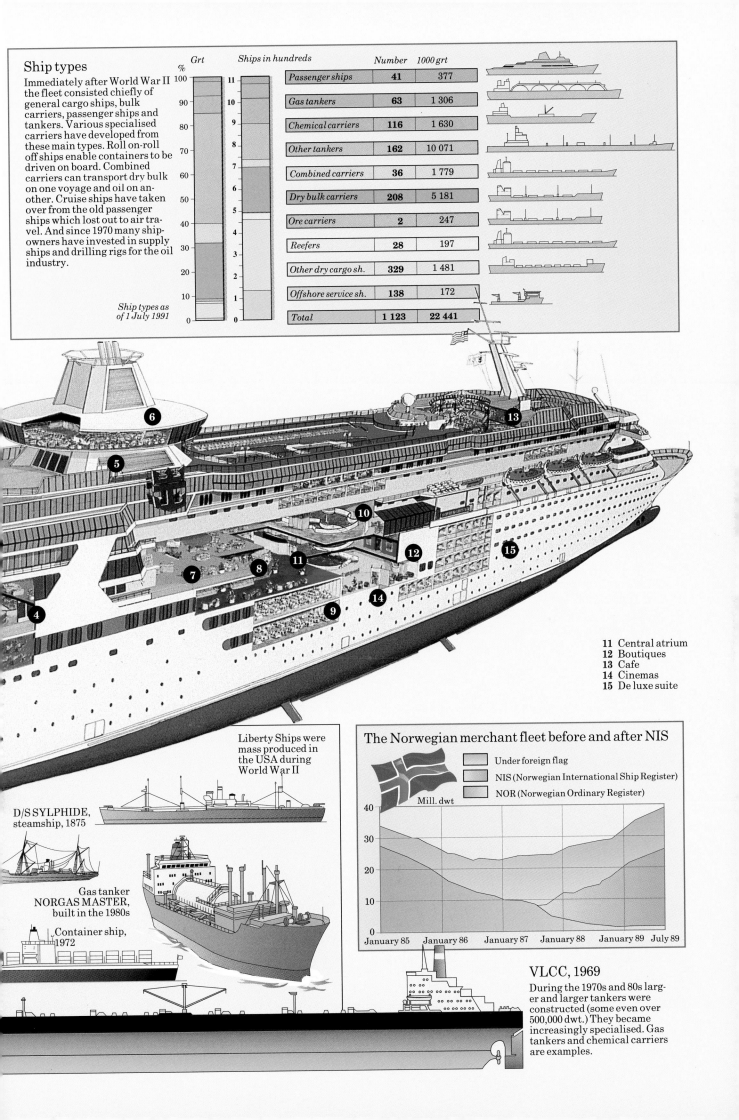

Ship types

Immediately after World War II the fleet consisted chiefly of general cargo ships, bulk carriers, passenger ships and tankers. Various specialised carriers have developed from these main types. Roll on-roll off ships enable containers to be driven on board. Combined carriers can transport dry bulk on one voyage and oil on another. Cruise ships have taken over from the old passenger ships which lost out to air travel. And since 1970 many ship-owners have invested in supply ships and drilling rigs for the oil industry.

Ship types as of 1 July 1991

	Grt %	Ships in hundreds		Number	1000 grt
Passenger ships				41	377
Gas tankers				63	1 306
Chemical carriers				116	1 630
Other tankers				162	10 071
Combined carriers				36	1 779
Dry bulk carriers				208	5 181
Ore carriers				2	247
Reefers				28	197
Other dry cargo sh.				329	1 481
Offshore service sh.				138	172
Total				1 123	22 441

11 Central atrium
12 Boutiques
13 Cafe
14 Cinemas
15 De luxe suite

D/S SYLPHIDE, steamship, 1875

Gas tanker NORGAS MASTER, built in the 1980s

Container ship, 1972

Liberty Ships were mass produced in the USA during World War II

The Norwegian merchant fleet before and after NIS

Under foreign flag
NIS (Norwegian International Ship Register)
NOR (Norwegian Ordinary Register)

Mill. dwt

40
30
20
10
0

January 85   January 86   January 87   January 88   January 89   July 89

VLCC, 1969

During the 1970s and 80s larger and larger tankers were constructed (some even over 500,000 dwt.) They became increasingly specialised. Gas tankers and chemical carriers are examples.

The situation was not made any easier when the price of oil dropped dramatically and foreign currency dealers began to sell Norwegian kroner. During the winter of 1985–86 the Bank of Norway spent NOK 28,000 millions supporting the krone. The balance of payments deficit grew and the Willoch government was forced to raise taxation and cut public expenditure. However, the Party of Progress, which held the balance in the Storting, could not accept an increase in petrol duties. When the Labour Party supported them, the government demanded a vote of confidence and was forced to resign.

The Labour Party formed a minority government, led by Gro Harlem Brundtland. It remained in power until the 1989 general election, after which a new non-socialist government was formed under Prime Minister Jan P. Syse (Conservative).

The Norwegian International Ship Register

In the 1980s Norwegian shipowners registered a growing number of vessels under flags of convenience, due to high costs in Norway and stronger international competition. Both the revenues from shipping and the number of Norwegian seamen fell alarmingly. Norway's maritime traditions and many land-based jobs were in danger of disappearing.

In the face of strong protests from the Norwegian Seamen's Union, the Storting passed a resolution establishing the Norwegian International Ship Register (NIS) in 1987. Through this register, shipowners could enter into wage agreements with foreign seamen without interference from Norwegian trade unions, thereby saving millions of kroner per vessel in crew costs.

The Register was a success. After only three years, over 850 ships accounting for a total of 38 million dwt were registered in NIS. Foreign exchange earnings from shipping rose again and the side-effects for maritime industries on land were considerable. In 1989 shipowners purchased goods and services from Norwegian companies for nearly NOK 10,000 millions. By the early 1990s Norway had become an international centre for shipbroking and maritime insurance.

The development of the NIS fleet was not without problems. Several serious accidents at sea raised questions of whether the oldest vessels had sufficiently high standards and whether the crews were well enough qualified. The authorities therefore expanded the Norwegian Ship Control, while the shipowners increased allocations for the training of officers.

The New Liberalism

When the Party of Progress was founded in 1972 its main aim was to achieve «a strong reduction in taxes, duties and official interference». The new party was inspired by a Danish anti-tax party and was an expression of dissatisfaction with the moderate policies of the Conservative Party. As the Conservatives increased cooperation with the centrist parties, the need devel-

From the mid-1980s Norwegian households were able to receive satellite broadcasts from foreign television stations.

oped for an alternative that would give more room for market forces and private initiative.

Until the mid-1980s between 1.9 and 6.3 percent of the electorate supported the Party of Progress. The party often suffered from internal disagreements and many people erroneously believed that it would disappear. At the 1987 local elections the Party of Progress received nationwide support and at the general election two years later it achieved 13 per cent of the vote.

People who supported the Party of Progress were not only tired of high taxation. They also opposed the way in which the government and the municipalities were taking over more and more responsibilities and using ever larger amounts of money. The party was inspired by the neo-liberalist policies of Margaret Thatcher and Ronald Reagan.

Norwegian neo-liberalism was a reaction against the welfare and equality policies that had been pursued since 1945. The Party of Progress believed that the public authorities had become too concerned with protecting and supporting ordinary people, and that individuals should be paid according to their contribution.

The party appealed to those who were against government aid to developing countries and critical of immigration from third world countries. People who were sceptical about the women's liberation movement were also likely to vote for the Party of Progress.

Much of the growing popularity of the Party of Progress was due to its leader, Carl I. Hagen. He had personal charm, spoke simply and clearly and made a good impression on television. Hagen represented a fresh, new style which appealed to people who had become tired of the old party-political wrangling.

Odd Nerdrum: «Social security», 1973.

Aquaculture

At the end of the nineteenth century pioneers began experimenting on hatching and breeding fish in Norway. They tried breeding trout and salmon in fresh water, but the venture eas not iverative. At the beginning or the 1970s, fish-farming in sea-water became a new growth industry. Fish are kept and fed in floating cages in the sea.

In 1973 the Storting determined that those wishing to establish a fish-farm had to have a licence. The politicians wanted installations to be distributed along the coast in order to create new industries in the outlying regions. Most fish-farms bred rainbow trout to start with, but since 1976 salmon has accounted for a large proportion of production. In the 1980s salmon production doubled every other year. The fish-farming industry, scientists and the authorities cooperate closely to prevent disease and pollution. The production of cod, halibut, char and turbot began at the end of the 1980s.

Many fish farms have modern computer equipment to control the water temperature and the feeding of fish.

In autumn the roe is extracted from female salmon. The roe is fertilised with milt from selected male fish. Farmed fish originates from Norwegian wild salmon.

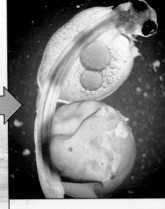

The fry leave the roe in the late winter. The first feeding begins after a few weeks. During the following year the fry develop into smolt (young fish).

When the fish (smolt) are one-and-a-half years old they are put into the sea. It is important that the fish have plenty of room to avoid damage. Fish-farmers have to ensure that there are no holes in the cages. Farmed fish should not mix with wild fish. After three or four years in the cages the salmon are ready for slaughter.

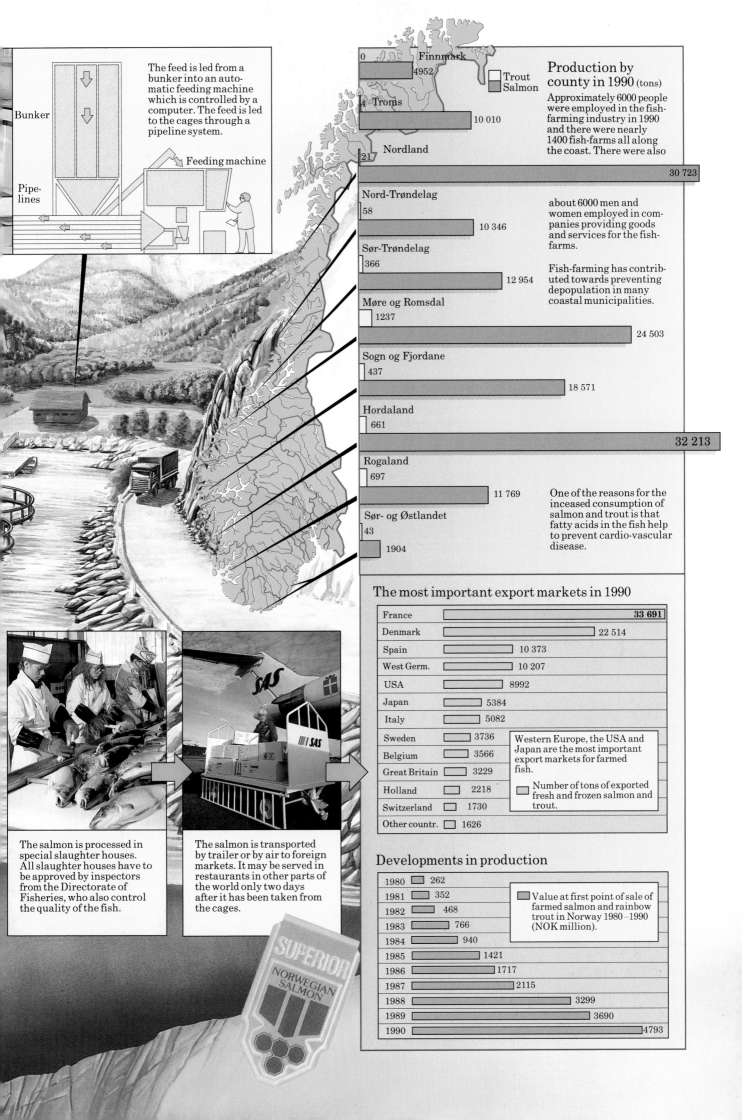

The feed is led from a bunker into an automatic feeding machine which is controlled by a computer. The feed is led to the cages through a pipeline system.

Bunker

Pipe-lines

Feeding machine

Production by county in 1990 (tons)

Approximately 6000 people were employed in the fish-farming industry in 1990 and there were nearly 1400 fish-farms all along the coast. There were also about 6000 men and women employed in companies providing goods and services for the fish-farms.

Fish-farming has contributed towards preventing depopulation in many coastal municipalities.

One of the reasons for the inceased consumption of salmon and trout is that fatty acids in the fish help to prevent cardio-vascular disease.

County	Trout	Salmon
Finnmark	0	4952
Troms	4	10 010
Nordland	21	30 723
Nord-Trøndelag	58	10 346
Sør-Trøndelag	366	12 954
Møre og Romsdal	1237	24 503
Sogn og Fjordane	437	18 571
Hordaland	661	32 213
Rogaland	697	11 769
Sør- og Østlandet	43	1904

Trout
Salmon

The salmon is processed in special slaughter houses. All slaughter houses have to be approved by inspectors from the Directorate of Fisheries, who also control the quality of the fish.

The salmon is transported by trailer or by air to foreign markets. It may be served in restaurants in other parts of the world only two days after it has been taken from the cages.

The most important export markets in 1990

Country	Tons
France	33 691
Denmark	22 514
Spain	10 373
West Germ.	10 207
USA	8992
Japan	5384
Italy	5082
Sweden	3736
Belgium	3566
Great Britain	3229
Holland	2218
Switzerland	1730
Other countr.	1626

Western Europe, the USA and Japan are the most important export markets for farmed fish.

Number of tons of exported fresh and frozen salmon and trout.

Developments in production

Year	Value
1980	262
1981	352
1982	468
1983	766
1984	940
1985	1421
1986	1717
1987	2115
1988	3299
1989	3690
1990	4793

Value at first point of sale of farmed salmon and rainbow trout in Norway 1980–1990 (NOK million).

SUPERIOR
NORWEGIAN SALMON

Symptoms of Crisis

At the beginning of the 1980s most people believed that poverty and distress had been eradicated in Norway. Social scientists soon found out that this was a myth. A survey carried out in 1985 showed that about 5 percent of the population – about 200,000 people – could be considered as «newly-poor». Most of these were elderly, single parents, disabled, or unemployed young people.

The newly-poor did not have to fight hunger, cold, malnutrition or infectious diseases as poor people had done in earlier times, but they had to struggle to find money for things that the majority did not have to worry about.

The number of people on disability pensions increased rapidly in the 1980s. One of the reasons was that older people had difficulty in adjusting to the new demands of working life. In 1987 one third of all Norwegians reaching retirement age were already on disability pensions.

Expenditure on social security benefits also increased and in 1987 it was 2.5 times higher than in 1980. The main reason for this was the marked rise in housing costs; in the 1980s an industrial worker had to pay approximately five years' income to

buy a new house; in the 1950s one year's income would have been enough.

The stock market crash in autumn 1987 sent shock waves through the business community. Share prices fell sharply and many businesses went into liquidation, particularly in the retail trade. Norwegian banks lost about NOK 13,000 millions in bad debts.

The Labour Party government introduced a number of measures to deflate the economy. With the help of higher taxes and interest rates and legislation to limit wage increases, they managed to curb both private consumption and price increases. The anti-inflationary policies were continued by the Syse government from autumn 1989 and by the beginning of the 1990s the competitive ability of Norwegian industry was improving. However there was one problem that had not been solved, namely unemployment. In autumn 1990 there were over 100,000 unemployed – the highest figure since the war.

In the 1980s the depopulation of northern Norway accelerated. Between 1980 and 1985 the number of inhabitants fell by about 10,000 and people continued to move out. The crisis in the fisheries was the main reason for these depressing figures.

In 1991 three women led political parties in Norway. From left to right, Kaci Kullmann Five, Conservative; Gro Harlem Brundtland, Labour; Anne Enger Lahnstein, Centre Party.

Norway on the Threshold of the Year 2000

At the beginning of the 1990s Norwegian politicians had still not learned to control the oil economy. They had become far too dependent on oil revenues, spending too much and investing too little in activities that could help business and industry in the face of international competition. The gap between production and consumption in Norway, excluding the oil industry, had become too wide.

Norway was also at a crossroads in the international arena. Together with the other remaining EFTA countries, Norway entered into negotiations with the EC on an agreement for comprehensive economic cooperation. The negotiations created problems between the non-socialist parties. The Conservatives wanted Norway to adapt to the EC internal market to the greatest possible extent, while the Centre Party wanted to retain as much national control as possible, particularly over agriculture and the fishing industry. Disagreement over the terms of the proposed treaty led to the resignation of the Syse government in autumn 1990.

Once again the Labour Party had to form a minority government, with Gro Harlem Brundtland as Prime Minister.

The Kvalsund bridge in Finnmark.

Norway and the World

Norway is a small, rich, democratic, industrialised country on the northern periphery of Europe. In 1990 the population was 4.2 million and 88 percent belonged to the Lutheran Church of Norway.

At the end of the 1980s the UN published a survey of living standards in 130 countries. The survey was intended to show where it was best to live and Norway came in sixth place. According to the survey, Norway differs from other countries particularly in the following areas:

- Norway has little land under cultivation and the inhabitants are scattered
- A large number of people have moved to towns and urban areas in the last thirty years
- Norway imports more food than most other European countries
- The per capita gross national product is high
- Incomes are fairly evenly distributed throughout the population
- Norway gives the largest amount of development aid per capita of all the western industrialised countries
- A large proportion of women are involved in politics
- Norwegians drink a relatively little alcohol

Norway's first woman Prime Minister, Gro Harlem Brundtland, is often called the «World's Minister of the Environment» In the 1980s she headed the UN Commission on Environment and Development.

Import value
NOK 236,051 million

Services 29,5%
- Other services 16 784
- Norwegian expenditure abroad 20 555
- Costs of oil activities 4 906
- Costs of shipping 27 467

Traditional goods 58,3%
- Electric power 33
- Industrial products 129 209
- Mining and minerals 2 276
- Agriculture, forestry and fishing 5 463
- Crude oil 588

Ships and platforms 12,2%
- Ships 25 813
- Oil and offshore equipment 2 957

Export value
NOK 262,086 million

Services 27,5%
- Other services 16 748
- Foreign expenditure in Norway 10 040
- Oil and offshore services 3286
- Freight revenues from shipping 42 026

Traditional goods 41,9%
- Electric power 788
- Industrial products 102 306
- Mining and minerals 1920
- Agriculture, forestry and fishing 4760

Oil and gas 28,1%
- Oil and gas 73 764

Ships and platforms 2.5 %
- NOK 6448 million

JAMAICA NOK 15,4

NICARAGUA NOK 153,6 m

In 1960 Norway became a member of the European Free Trade Association, EFTA. Thirteen years later, Norway signed a free trade agreement with the EC.

Iceland
NORWAY
Finland
Sweden
Denmark
Great Br.
Ireland
Belgium
Lux.
The Netherl.
Germany
Austria
France
Switzerland
Portugal
Italy
Spain
Greece

☐ EFTA countries
▨ EC countries

500 km

Norwegian imports

This illustration shows the distribution of Norwegian imports from the continents of the world in 1989.

Europe: 75.74 %
N. America: 11.81 %
Asia: 8.16 %
Africa: 1.45 %
S. America: 2.39 %
Oceania: 0.45 %

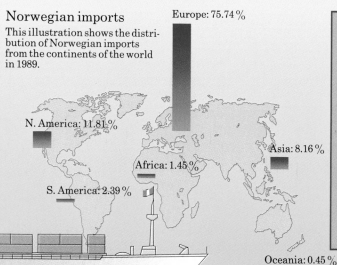

Imports from Europe in 1989

	%	0 1 2 3 4 5 6 7 8 9 10 11 12 13 14 15 16 17 18 19 20
Sweden		18,0
W. Germany		14,4
Great Britain		8,7
Holland		3,9
France		3,8
Finland		3,6
Italy		3,4
Belgium/Lux		2,9
Switzerland		1,7
Soviet Union		1,3
Spain		1,1

Imports from Asia in 1989

Japan	4,7
Taiwan	0,74
Hong Kong	0,72
China	0,65

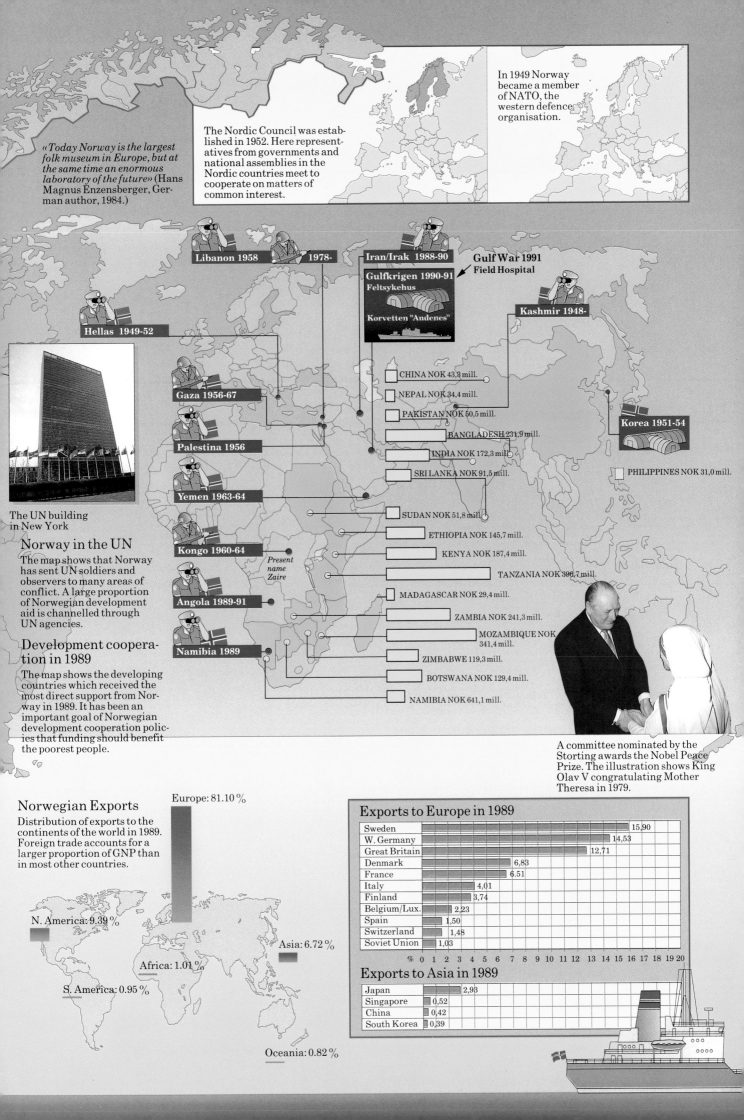

In 1949 Norway became a member of NATO, the western defence organisation.

The Nordic Council was established in 1952. Here representatives from governments and national assemblies in the Nordic countries meet to cooperate on matters of common interest.

«Today Norway is the largest folk museum in Europe, but at the same time an enormous laboratory of the future» (Hans Magnus Enzensberger, German author, 1984.)

Libanon 1958 1978-
Iran/Irak 1988-90
Gulf War 1991 Field Hospital
Gulfkrigen 1990-91 Feltsykehus
Korvetten "Andenes"
Kashmir 1948-
Hellas 1949-52
Gaza 1956-67
Palestina 1956
Yemen 1963-64
Kongo 1960-64
Present name Zaire
Angola 1989-91
Namibia 1989
Korea 1951-54

CHINA NOK 43,3 mill.
NEPAL NOK 34,4 mill.
PAKISTAN NOK 50,5 mill.
BANGLADESH 231,9 mill.
INDIA NOK 172,3 mill.
SRI LANKA NOK 91,5 mill.
PHILIPPINES NOK 31,0 mill.
SUDAN NOK 51,8 mill.
ETHIOPIA NOK 145,7 mill.
KENYA NOK 187,4 mill.
TANZANIA NOK 396,7 mill.
MADAGASCAR NOK 29,4 mill.
ZAMBIA NOK 241,3 mill.
MOZAMBIQUE NOK 341,4 mill.
ZIMBABWE 119,3 mill.
BOTSWANA NOK 129,4 mill.
NAMIBIA NOK 641,1 mill.

The UN building in New York

Norway in the UN

The map shows that Norway has sent UN soldiers and observers to many areas of conflict. A large proportion of Norwegian development aid is channelled through UN agencies.

Development cooperation in 1989

The map shows the developing countries which received the most direct support from Norway in 1989. It has been an important goal of Norwegian development cooperation policies that funding should benefit the poorest people.

A committee nominated by the Storting awards the Nobel Peace Prize. The illustration shows King Olav V congratulating Mother Theresa in 1979.

Norwegian Exports

Distribution of exports to the continents of the world in 1989. Foreign trade accounts for a larger proportion of GNP than in most other countries.

Europe: 81.10 %
N. America: 9.39 %
Asia: 6.72 %
Africa: 1.01 %
S. America: 0.95 %
Oceania: 0.82 %

Exports to Europe in 1989

	%
Sweden	15,90
W. Germany	14,53
Great Britain	12,71
Denmark	6,83
France	6.51
Italy	4,01
Finland	3,74
Belgium/Lux.	2,23
Spain	1,50
Switzerland	1,48
Soviet Union	1,03

% 0 1 2 3 4 5 6 7 8 9 10 11 12 13 14 15 16 17 18 19 20

Exports to Asia in 1989

	%
Japan	2,93
Singapore	0,52
China	0,42
South Korea	0,39

FOR FURTHER READING

T. K. Derry: A Short History of Norway. London 1968

T. K. Derry: A History of Modern Norway, 1814–1972. London 1973

R. Popperwell: Norway. London 1972.

John Midgaard: A Brief History of Norway, Oslo 1986.

T. Bergh, T. Hanisch, E. Lange and H. Pharo: Growth and Development. Oslo 1981.

P. Sveaas Andersen: Vikings of the West. The Expansion of Norway in the Middle Ages. Oslo 1985.

J. Brøndsted: The Vikings. London 1970.

M. Magnusson: Vikings! London 1970.

Snorri Sturluson: From the Sagas of the Norse Kings. Oslo 1984.

J. Andenæs, O. Riste and M. Skodvin: Norway and the Second World War. Oslo 1983.

J. G. Arntzen and B. B. Knudsen: Political Life and Institutions in Norway. Oslo 1981.

O. S. Lovoll: The Promise of America. A History of the Norwegian-American People. Minneapolis and Oslo 1984.

I. Semmingsen: Norway to America. A History of the Migration. Minneapolis 1980.

In 1990 the EC and EFTA sponsored The European Year of Turism contest for the best kept village. The international jury voted Lyngør in southern Norway the winner in March 1991.

ILLUSTRATIONS

The midnight sun at North Cape.

INDEX